Beauty to Embrace in an Afternoon

The Art of C. Sperry Andrews III at Weir Farm

Beauty to Embrace in an Afternoon

The Art of C. Sperry Andrews at Weir Farm

ISBN 979-8-9938945-2-2

Printed in the United States of America

First Edition

Dedication

In loving memory of my father, mother and brother and in appreciation of all the staff who have served at Weir Farm National Historical Park, especially Dolores.

Table of Contents

This book presents a curated selection of works conceived and created at Weir Farm from approximately 1955 to 1995. The artworks are arranged thematically rather than chronologically to highlight the range of his métier. The title is taken from a letter he wrote the year my parents acquired the farm and studios, reproduced on page eight.

My aim has been to honor his work, preserve his legacy, and make his art accessible again, as much of it has remained out of public view for many years. The absence of formal artistic training on my part likely shaped my editorial decisions in ways I hope are sympathetic to the spirit of his work.

To introduce his work to readers who may not know him, I have included material from his personal archives—notes, diaries, letters—and remembrances shared at his memorial service. Citations distinguish between these sources: eulogies are attributed by author, while personal documents (notes, diaries, and letters) are identified by date only. Because most works are undated and rarely titled, the index provides simple descriptions along with media and dimensions.

Acknowledgements

The recollections quoted in these pages helped shape the structure of this book, and I am grateful to all the voices who contributed. From 2003–2005 I engaged Marc Chabot to organize, preserve and begin cataloging the collection of oils. As the scope of the project became clear, Pat Hegenauer was engaged and photographed hundreds of additional works on paper. My brother Sperry collaborated with Marc to curate a representative selection spanning my father's entire career, several of which are featured in this volume.

I wish to thank Katie Knapp, Mike Magnotti, and Steve Bradbury for reviewing drafts of the book and offering both feedback and encouragement. I am grateful to Sabrina Crewe for providing the image on page 80, and to Elizabeth Poland (NPS) for discovering the letter "Why I Would Like to Be an Artist" in the park archives and for providing high-resolution images of several works in the NPS collection.

Why I would like to be an Artist

Our own United States is a beautiful country, with a strong spirit, which runs throughout the land. You can sense it on a bright morning in the Spring, Summer, Fall, and Winter.

You can see it in our people, in our farm lands, our cities. You can rejoice and be inspired by it.

Our own state of Connecticut is rich with beauty and spirit, a kind of close beauty that's small enough to embrace in an afternoon. Not spectacular our state, like some of our Western ranches, but gentleness, hills which are a synthesis with the countryside. Think of it. An afternoon by the pond, things that go with the time of season in accord.

I like to paint from these things, where I work out-doors on the sight. I like to get to know the countryside like a friend, and through this familiarity comes understanding, the more we know it the more we can enjoy it.

I think it is very strong this harmony, the intimate beauty of our Connecticut landscape. A painter finds here the Bluebird in his own back yard. Seek no further, I think there's an annual grown in the state by that name.

The credo for the artist:
(Go where the heart goes
If we only could recapture
the first careless rapture.)

Sperry Andrews
Ridgefield, Connecticut
May 24, 1958

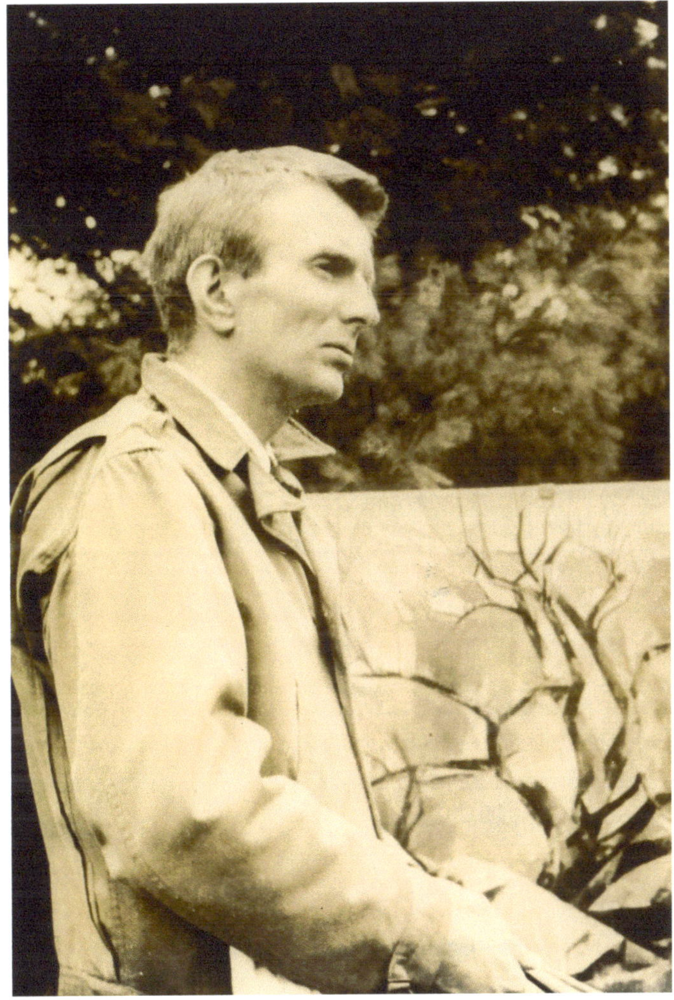

Why I would like to
be an Artist.

Our own United States is a
beautiful country. with a strong
spirit, which runs throughout
the land. You can sense it on
a bright morning in the Spring,
Summer, Fall and Winter.

You can see it in our people,
in our farm lands, our cities,
You can rejoice and be inspired
by it.

Our own State of Connecticut
is rich with beauty and spirit,
a kind of close beauty that's
small enough to embrace in
an afternoon, Not spectacular
our State, like some of our
Western Ranches, but gentleness,
hills which are a synthesis
with the country side. Think of
it. — An afternoon by the
pond, things that go with the
time of season in accord —

I like to paint from these
things, where I work out-dors
on the sight. I like to get to
know the country-side like a
friend and through this
familiarity comes understanding,
the more we know it the more
we can enjoy it.

I think it is very strong this
harmony, the intimate beauty
of our Connecticut landscape. A
painter finds here, the Blue-
Bird —) in his own back-yard
Seek no further, I think there's
an annual grown in the state
by that name.

(the credo for the artist
(So where the heart goes)
If we only could recapture
the first careless rapture.)

Perry Andrews
Ridgefield
Connecticut
May 24 1958

8

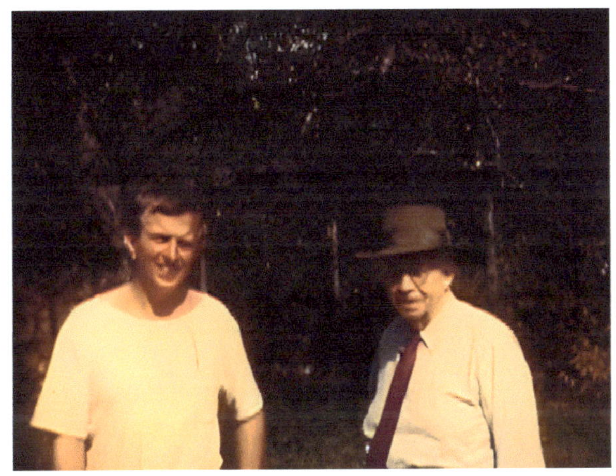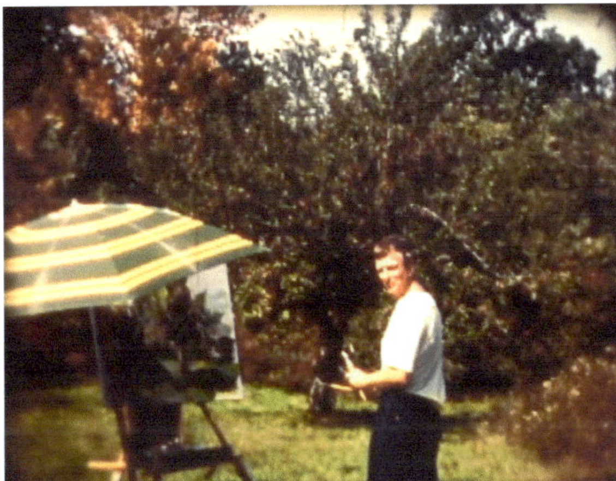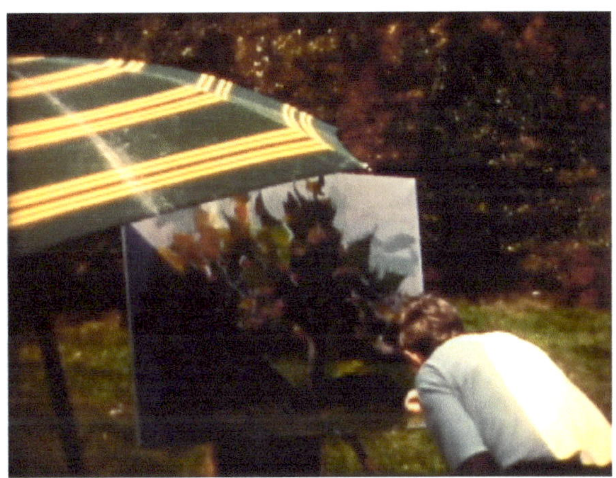

Sperry told me of an elderly artist called Mahonri Young who was living in Branchville. The next afternoon Sperry and I went to call on him. That proved to be the first of many meetings at Weir Farm. Sperry became a regular visitor and, when back at home in Wilton, I would join him. As my interest in painting and drawing grew, Sperry was encouraging and helpful in all sorts of ways. He taught me how to stretch a canvas, he advised me on materials, he would comment on whatever I was doing and always he set a fine example of how an artist lives and works. Sperry and I would discuss at length painting and the painters we both admired, making pilgrimages to the Hudson River to visit F.W. Church's home. Sperry was certainly eccentric, which was part of his considerable charm. He was a hilarious storyteller and the best of companions. I recall Sperry's excitement when, after purchasing Weir Farm, he went up to the attic to see if it was really possible to see the Danbury Hills, as Mr. Young had claimed. Well, it was and I still have a drawing he made titled 'Yes you can, you can still see the Danbury Hills!' (J. Hubbard, personal communication, August 2005).

Learn to think in a crisis: this takes many years of life. However, too much thinking takes the edge off the first excitement, which means a lot for the fresh quality one desires. One cannot expect too much, but if the attack is strong and direct, your efforts will have heart. (Notes, May 9, 1977).

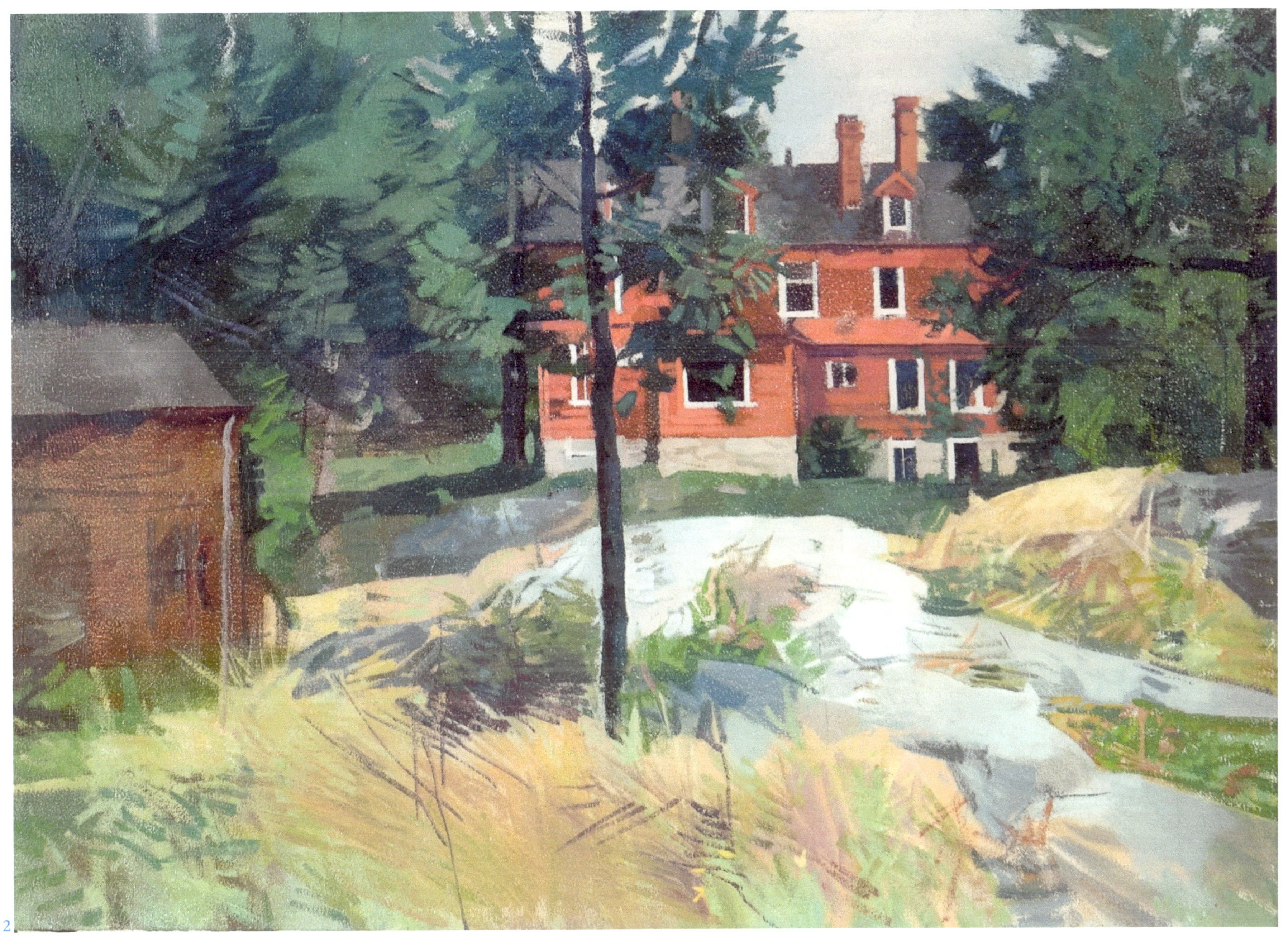

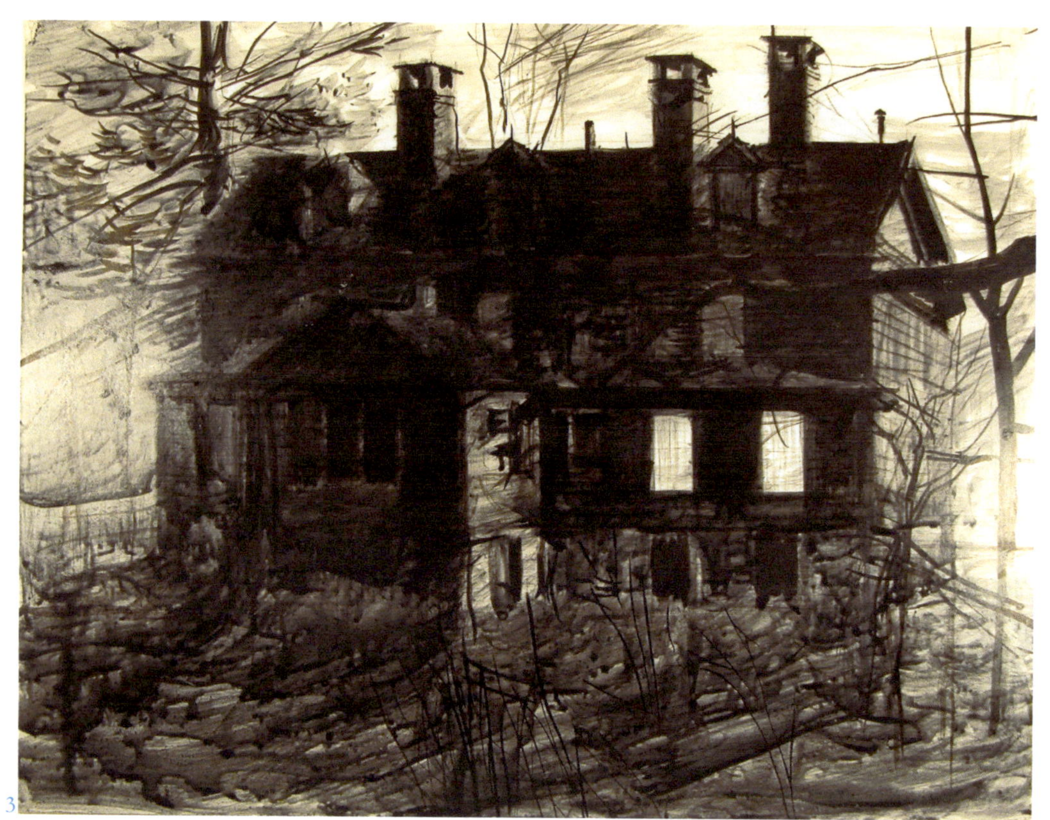

3

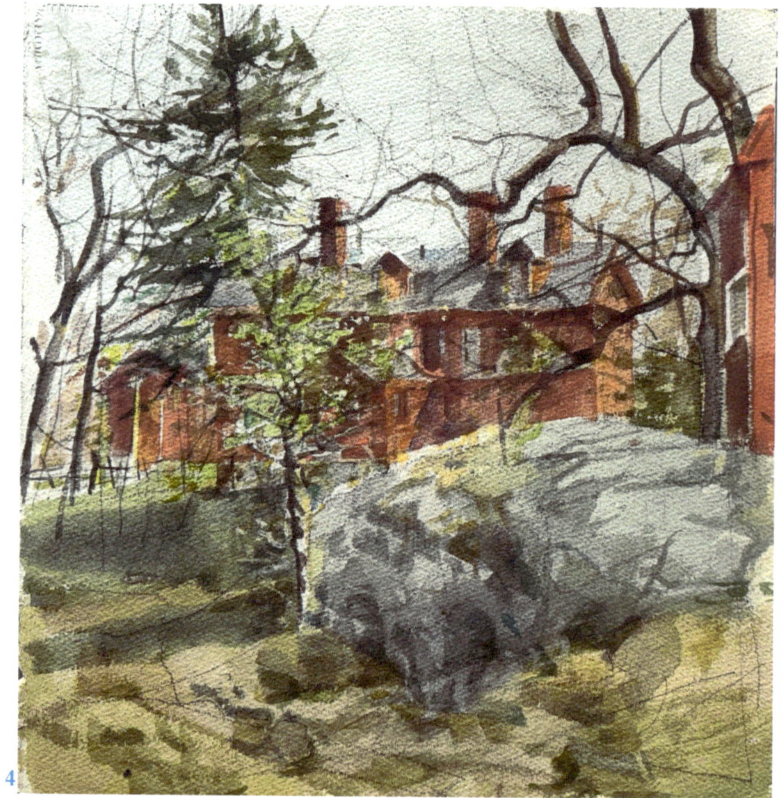

4

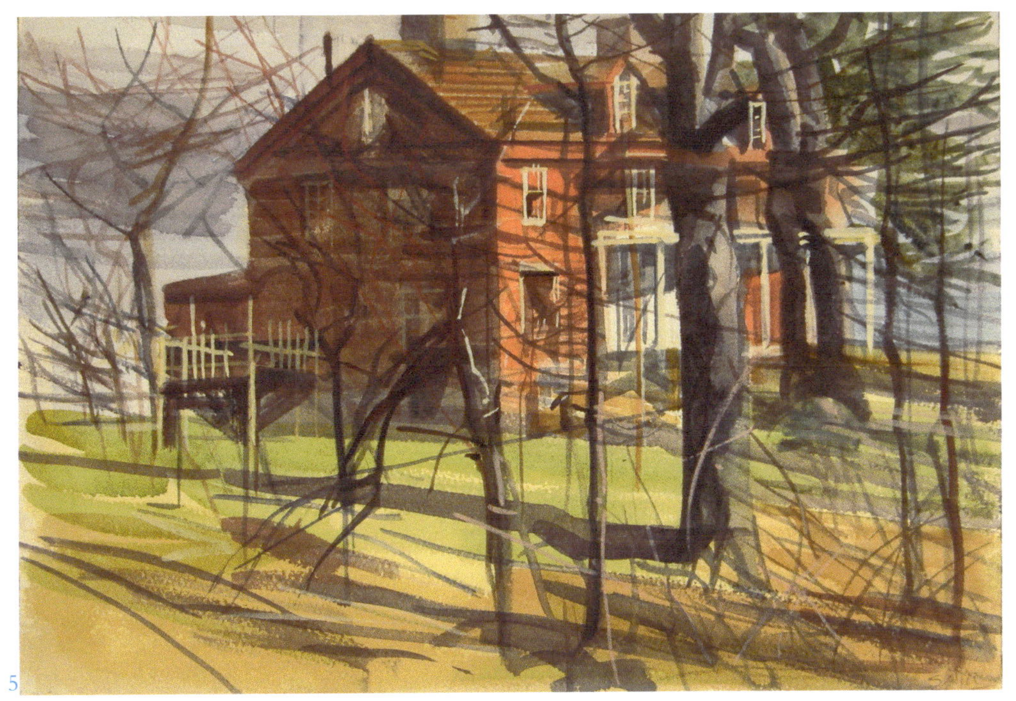

5

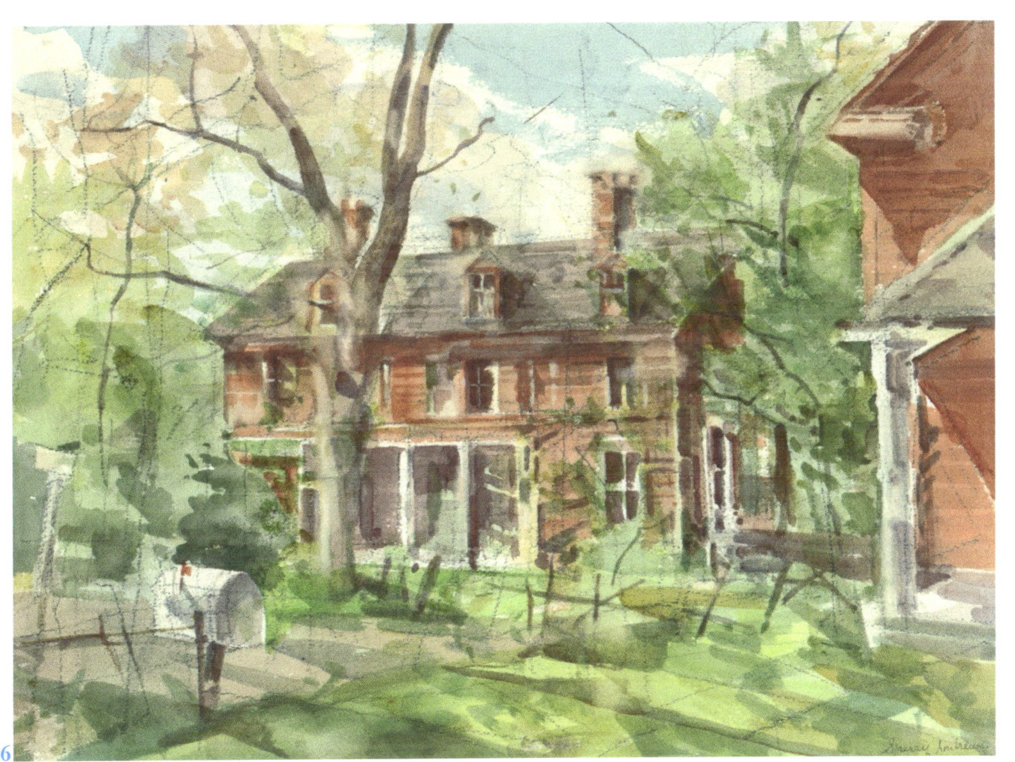

6

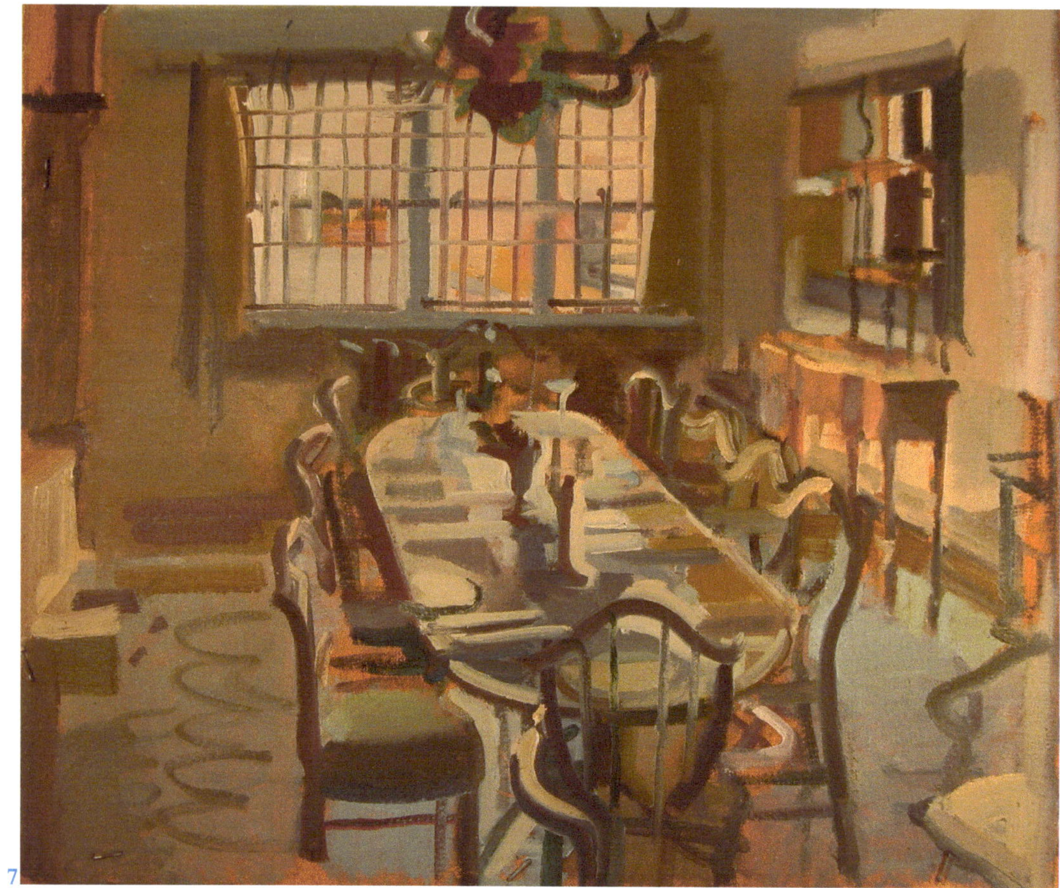 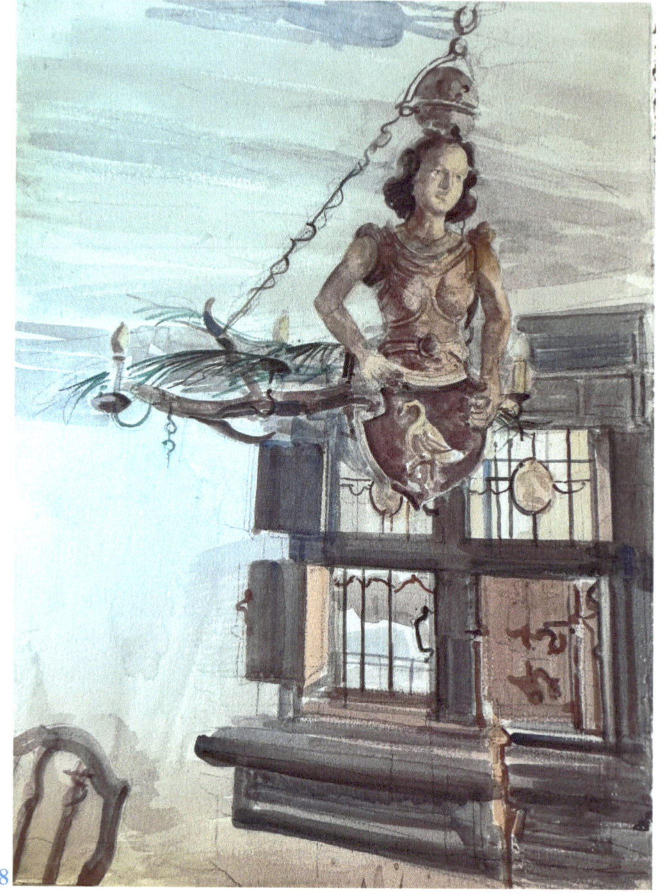

The dining room was immense. I remember the antler chandeliers. I remember both Doris and Sperry telling stories about the different pieces of furniture in the room. But mostly I remember the vibrancy of the people. The table was filled with artists and writers and actors. Young people and old people, wonderful giving people who had interesting lives and were willing to share their stories. All of us had a real love for Doris and Sperry. The evenings were special. I remember once it was about two o'clock in the morning and no one had budged from the table. Not because there was a lot of alcohol but because the conversation was so full and rich no one wanted to leave.
(C. Gibbons, personal communication, August 29, 2005)

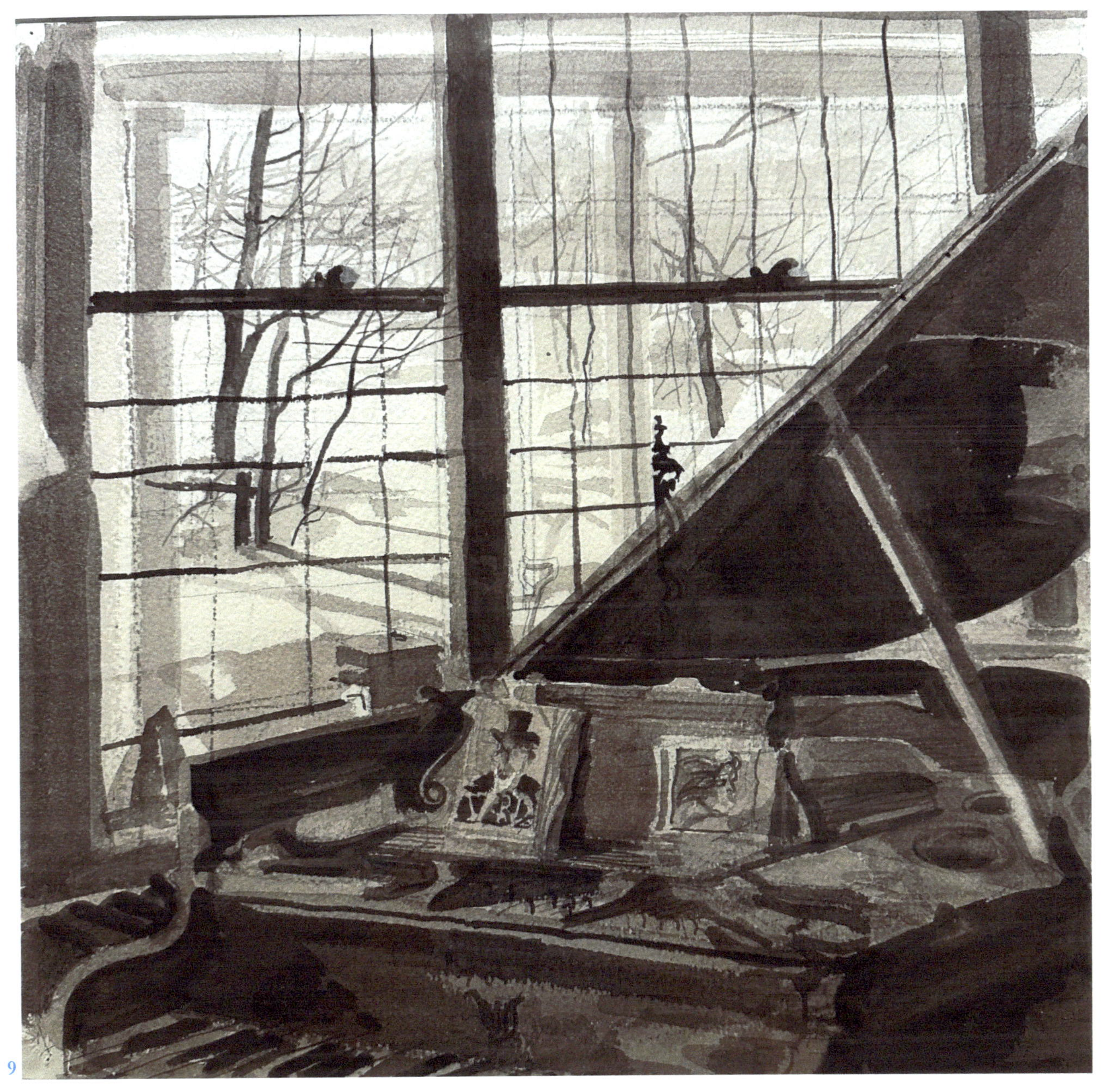

I am very proud of your desire to do with your life what you wish to do in your heart. I have enjoyed this privilege. It can be very rewarding at times. (Letter to the author, November 10, 1974)

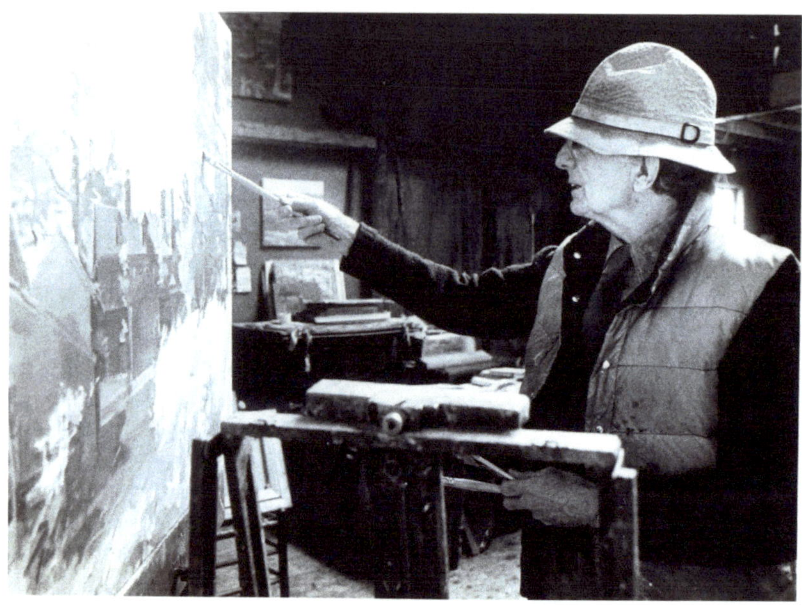

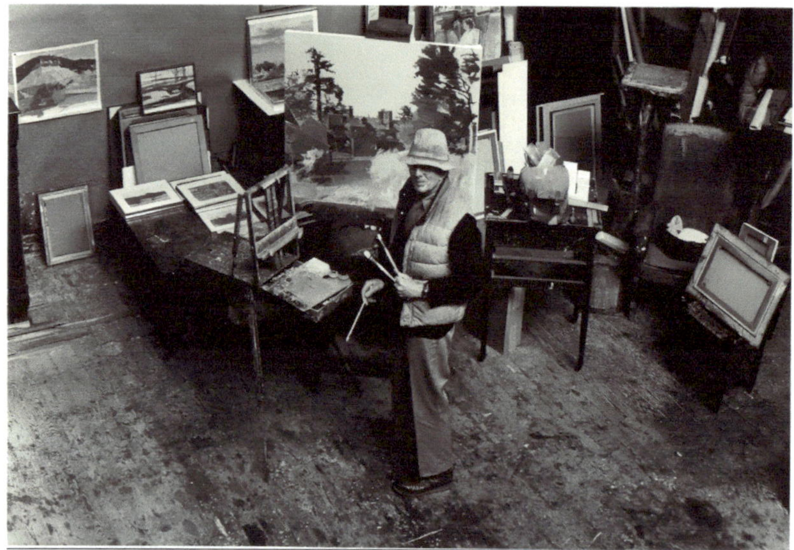

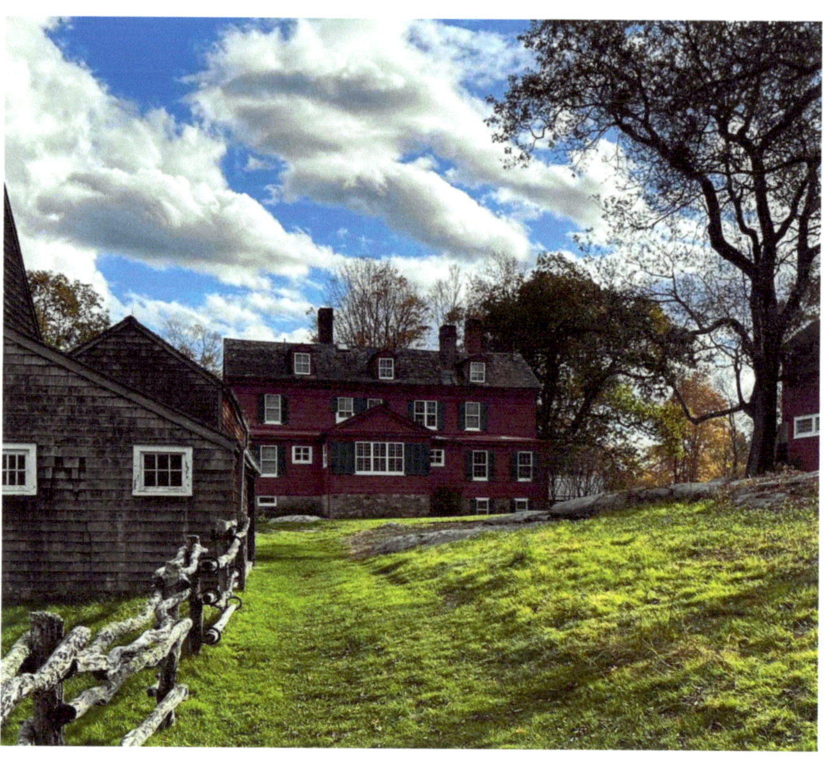

To see Sperry paint is what being an artist is all about. He had found something beautiful that had captured his attention. His focus was complete. He was totally in the beauty of the moment. I knew then that I had the privilege of being in the presence of a real artist. (C. Gibbons, private communication, August 2005)

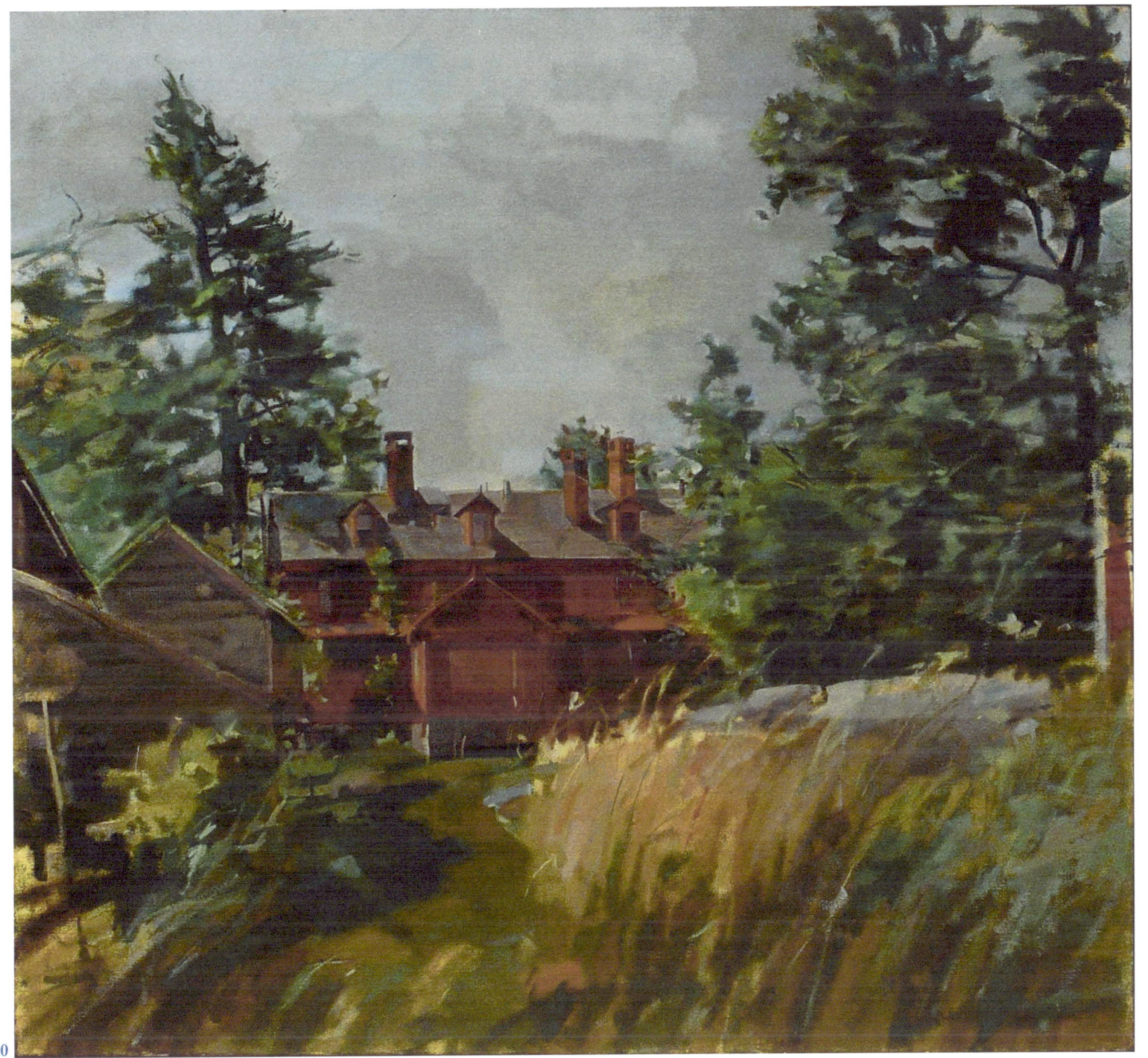

10

Yard

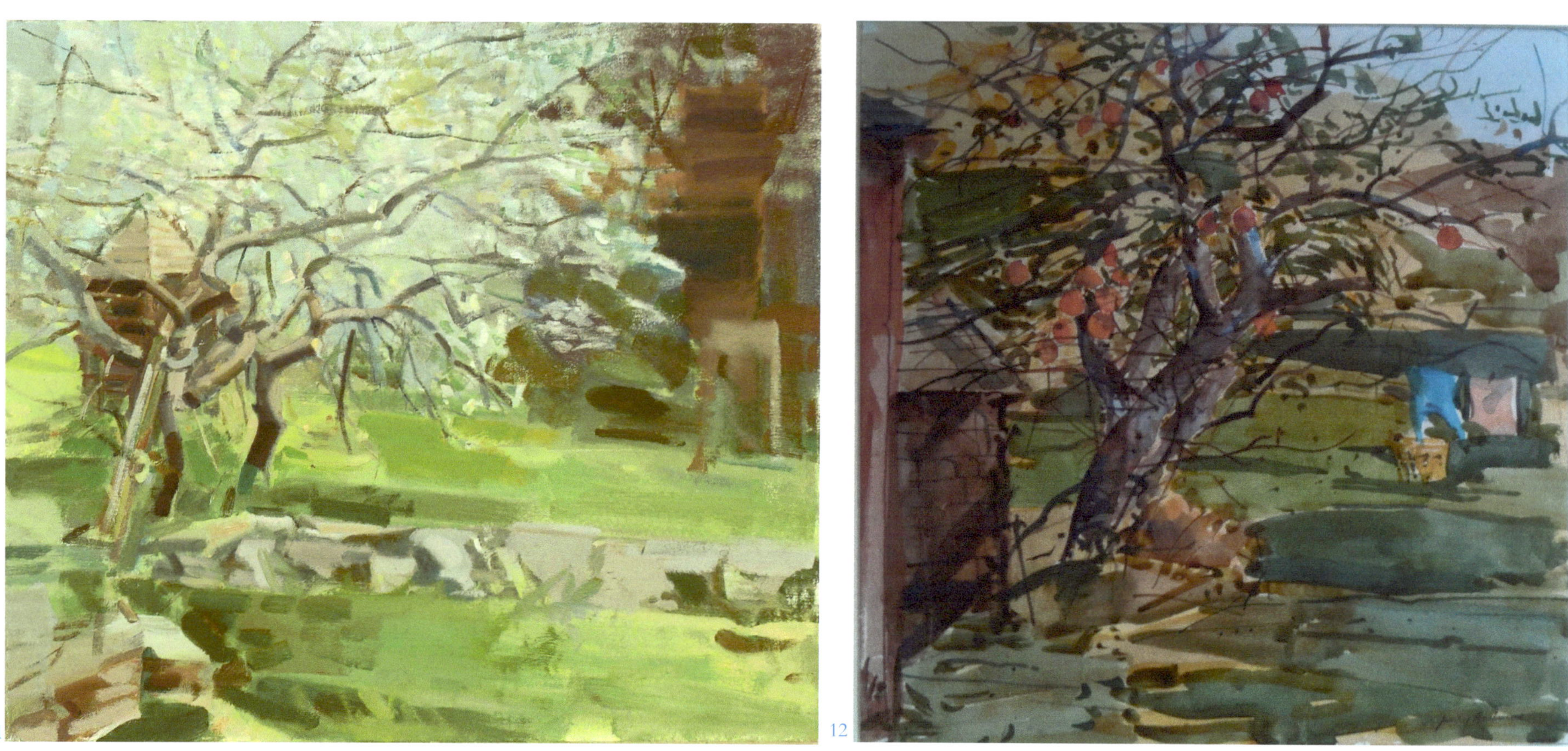

Don't have others on your mind. Learn to think only of that moment and how much it means to you (notes, April 6, 1977).

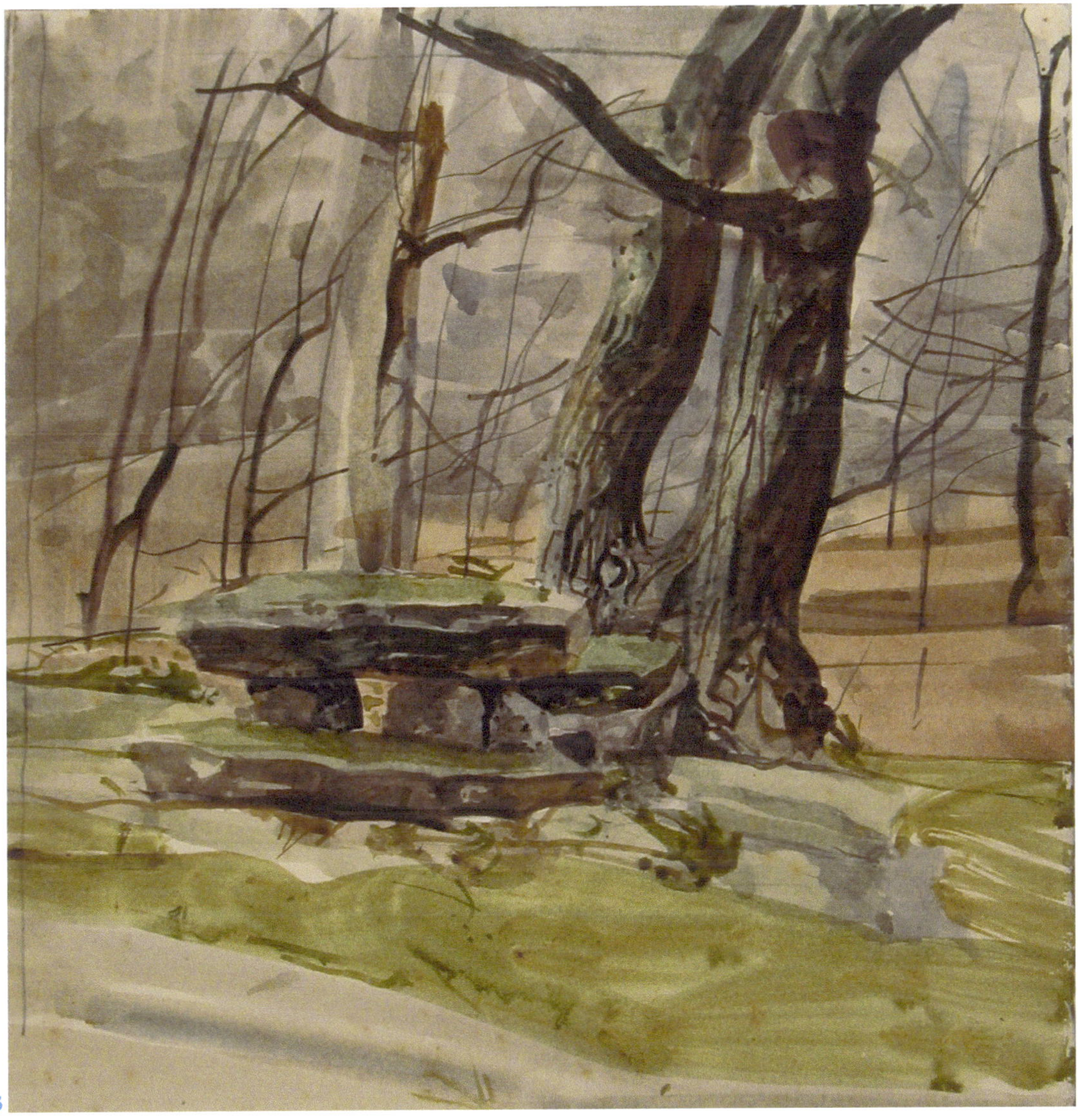

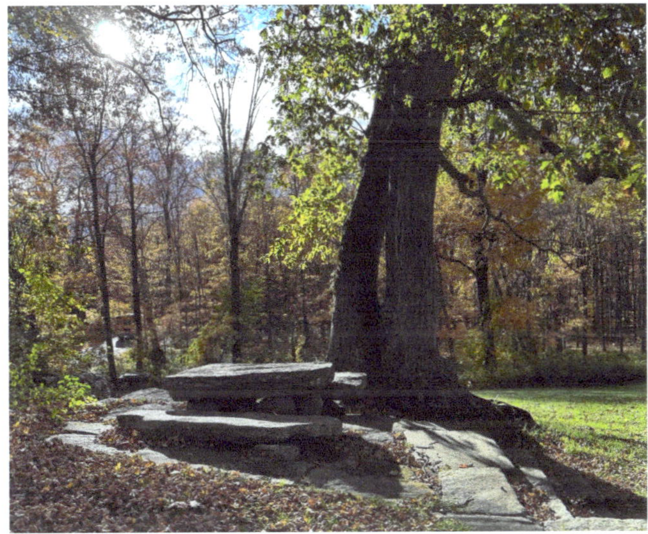

Preparation for the immediate attack or action is essential for this kind of working. One can train the eye for the plan ahead. Often the best results are the result of quick action. To think may waste away the moment (notes, November 27, 1978).

14

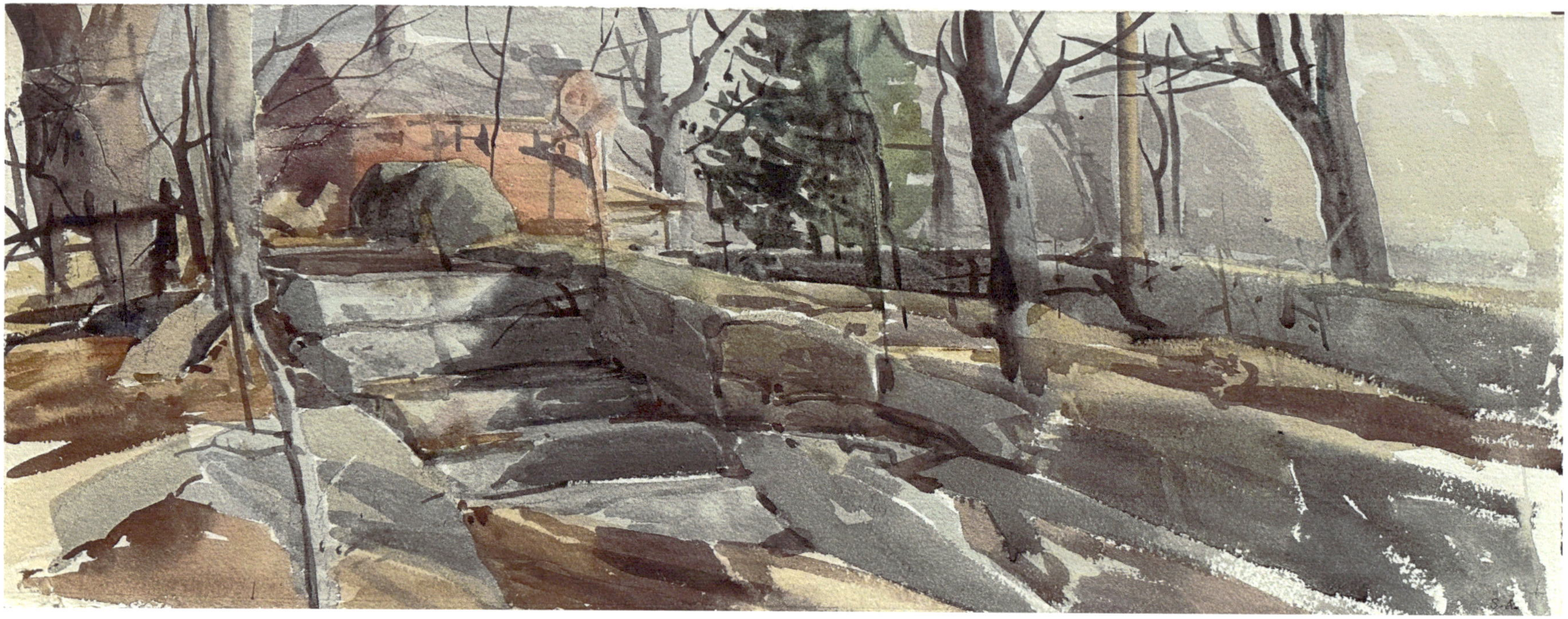

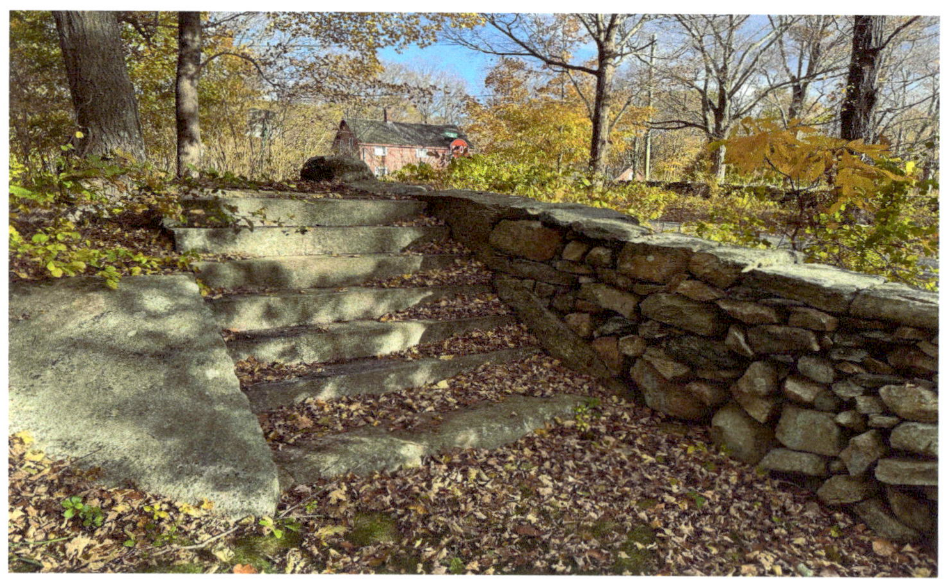

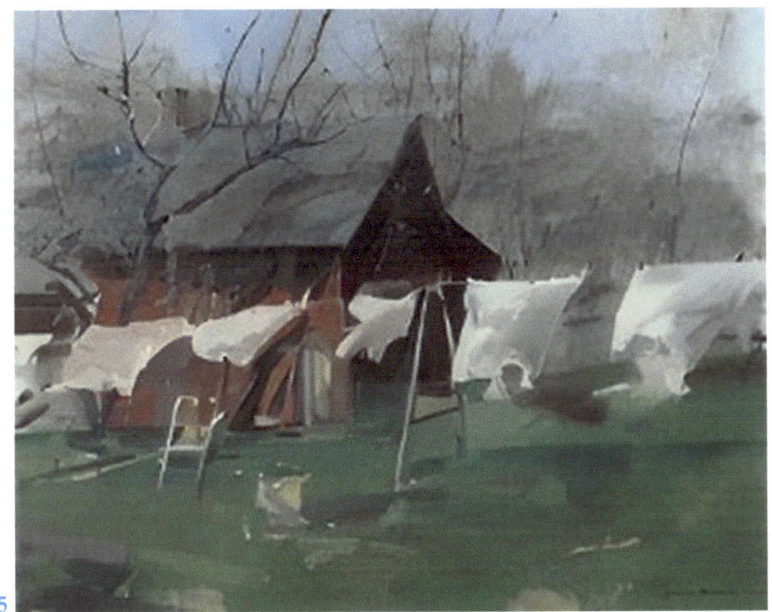

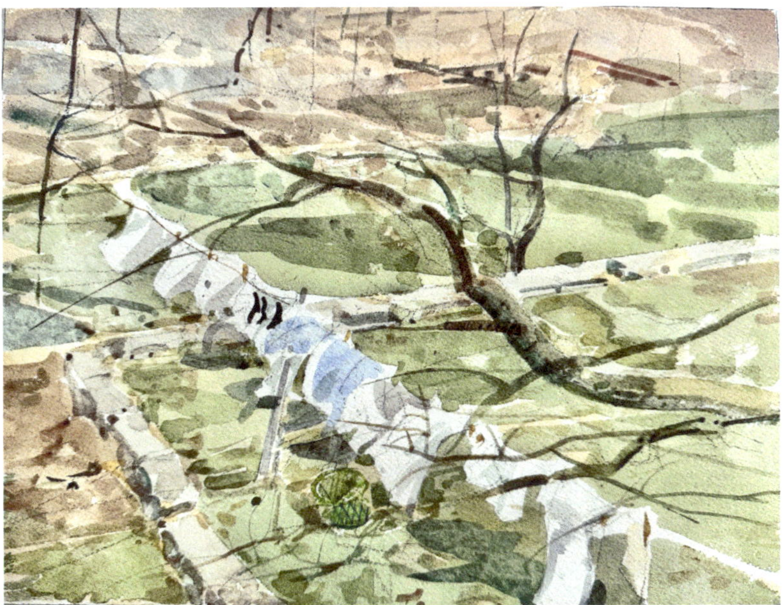

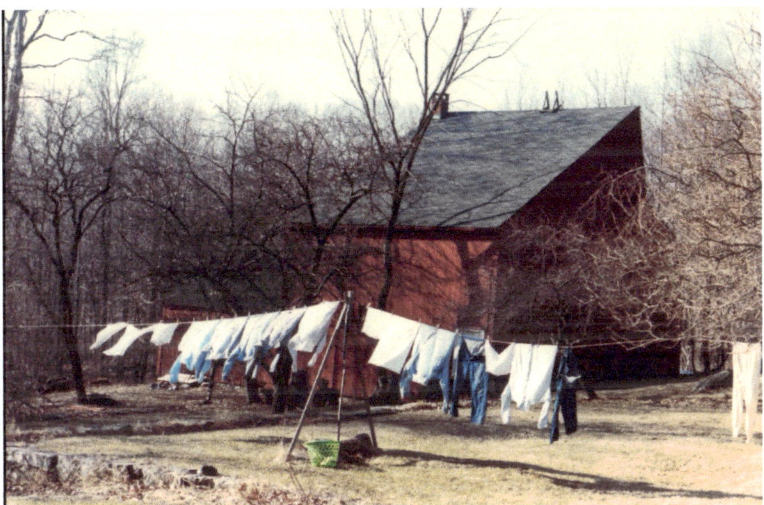

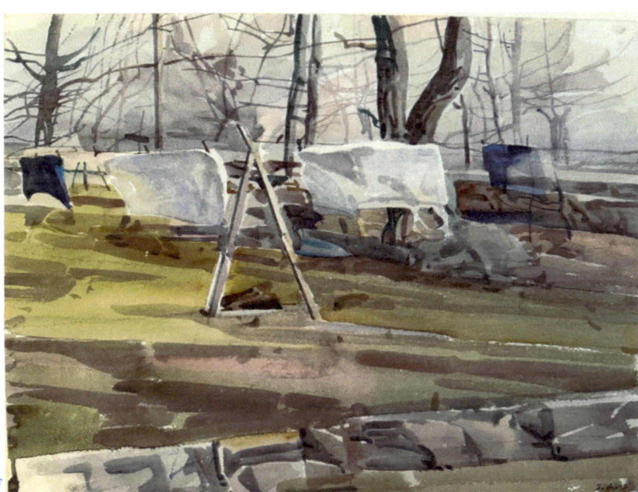

On a fine summer day in the early 1970s, Sperry Andrews, who had painted at this spot for many years, invited me to come along and paint with him. This was truly an honor, a golden opportunity. I decided to do a study of the laundry blowing in the wind on the clothes line. An inspiring teacher, Sperry Andrews shared so many valuable thoughts and ideas about painting. With great humor and a love of life, he let me know his feelings about his work as an artist. We had fun that day admiring the beauty all around us and painting it (K. Knapp, Block Island, 2007).

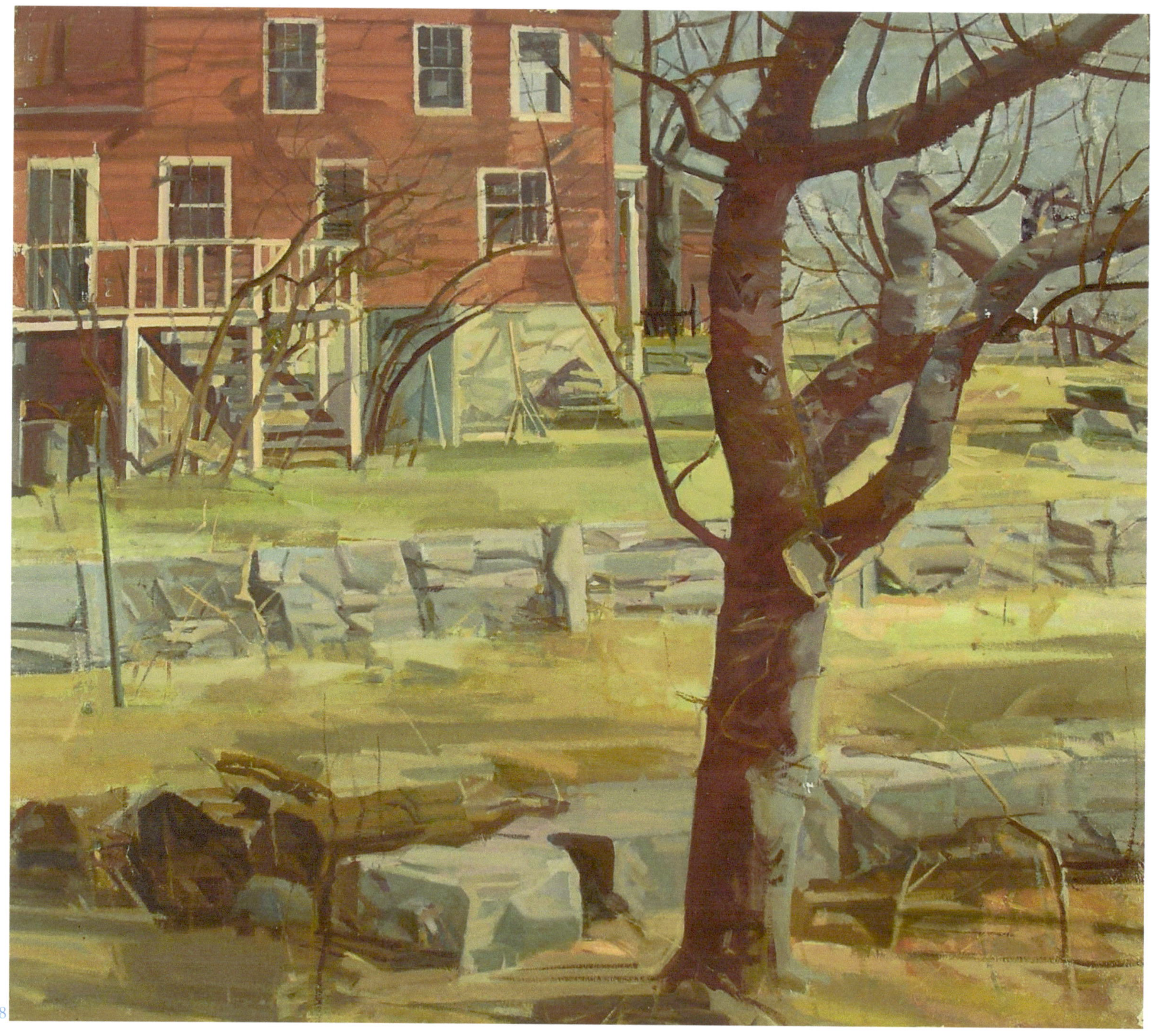

18

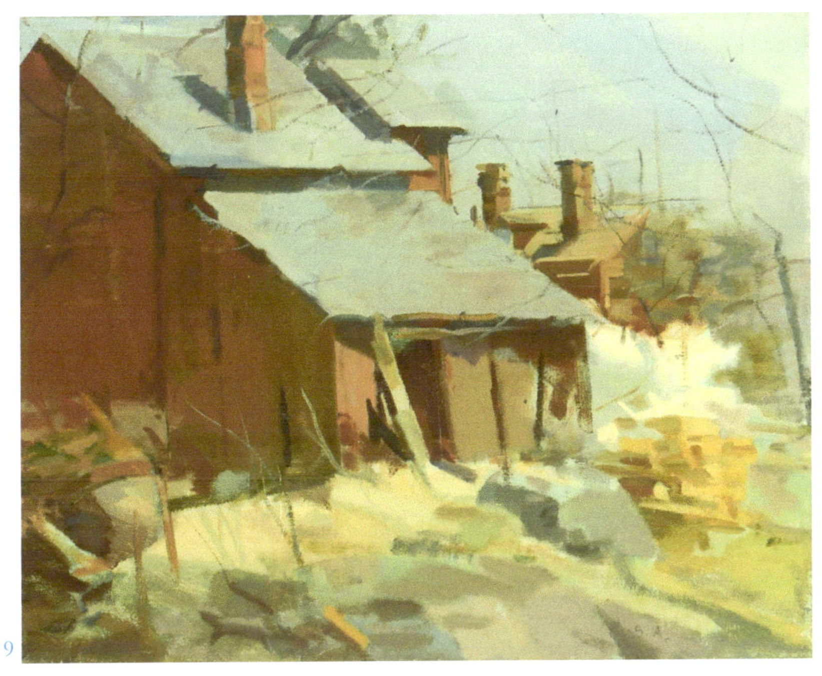

19

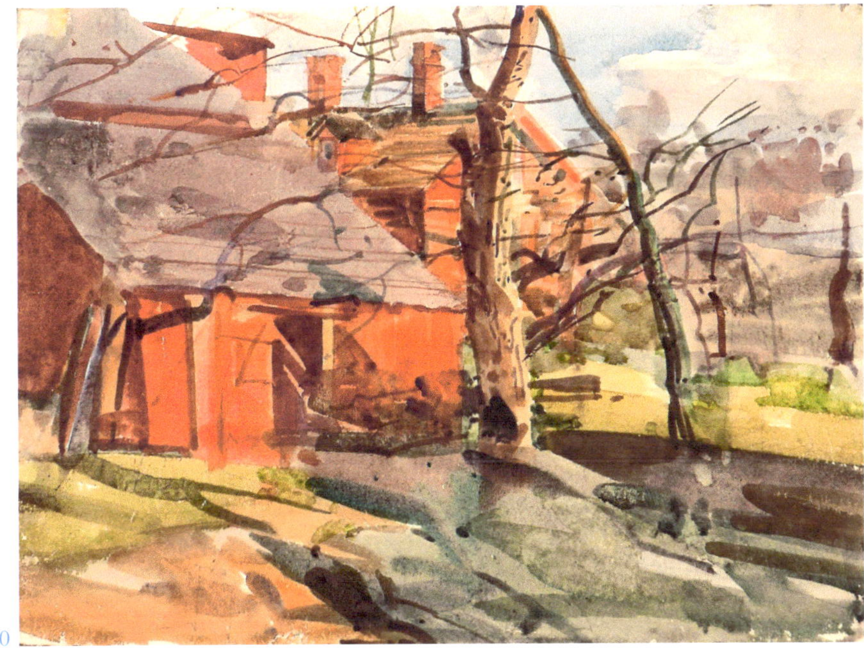

20

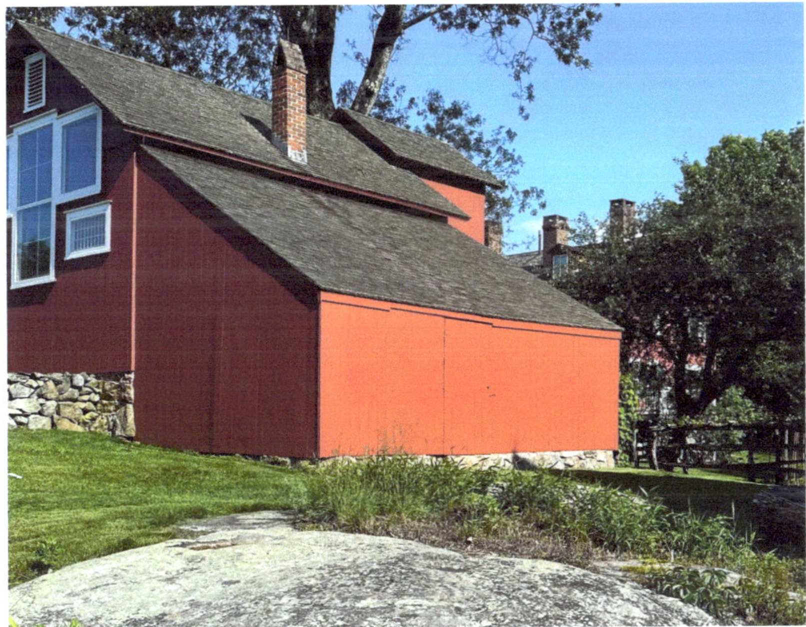

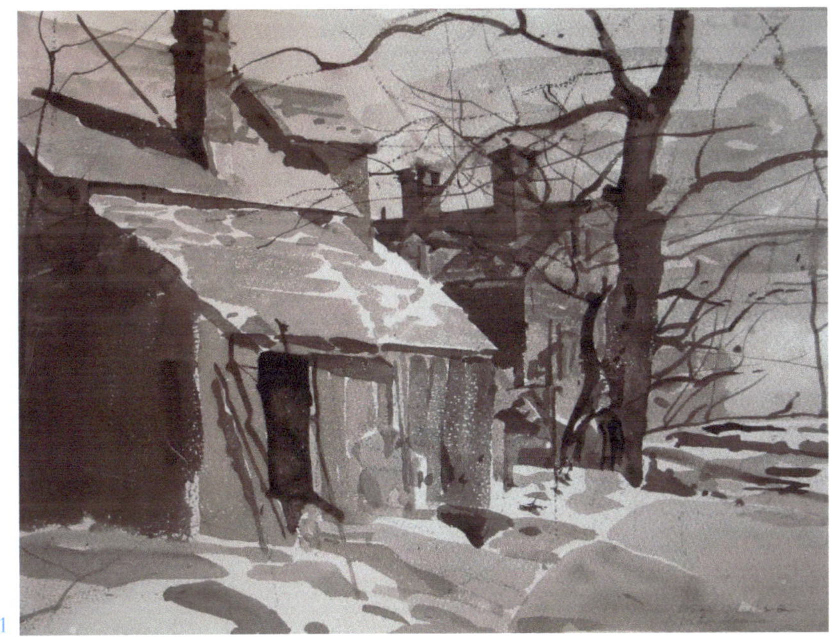

21

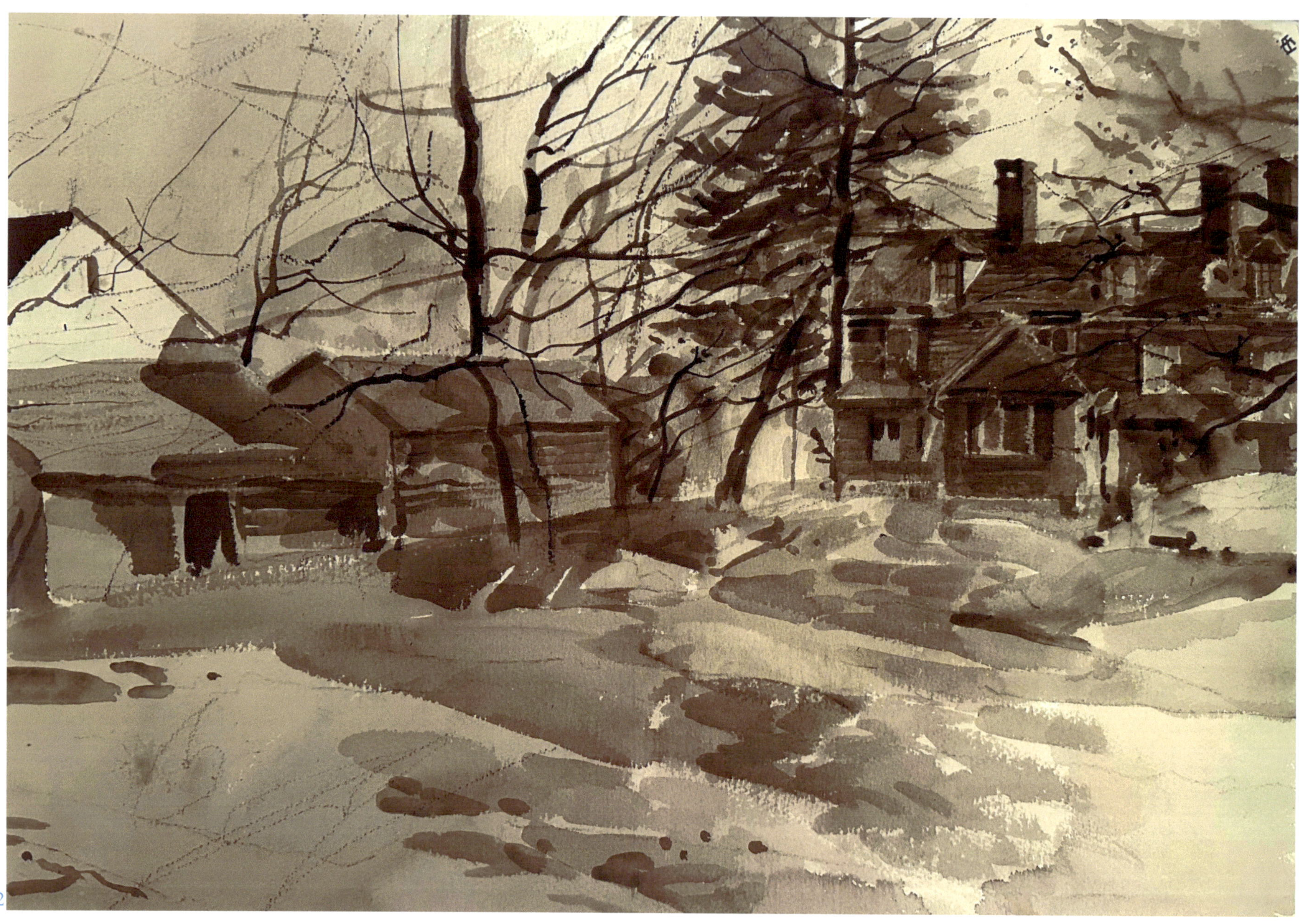

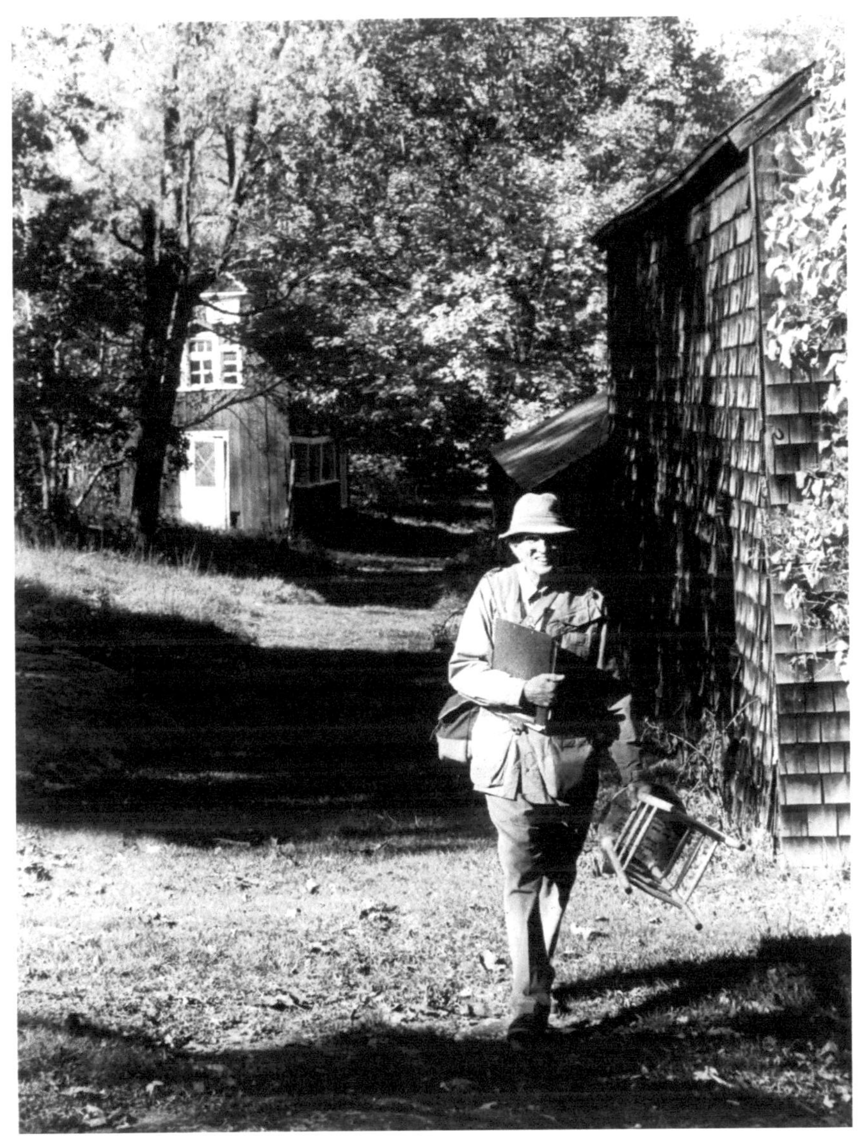

Being with your father was a continuously wonderful experience and one from which I always gain so much insight into another way of looking at everything. Thank God for true individuals. Taking a walk with Sperry was a truly stimulating experience. It was a look into a world that he could articulate so clearly, most clearly, with a paintbrush. He opened up a trip that I had no idea I was in for, totally unexpected that he would help me to see what I had seen often, but not really seen. Sperry looked way beyond the surface, which took more energy than the average person could begin to muster up. Of course, he was a painter. Light texture, surface color shape, that was his world. All of a sudden, he made you aware of a whole new set of dimensions that could have been so easily missed. The obvious didn't escape him. For him, it was right there all the time. Sperry was much more discerning than anyone might suspect, which was part of the intrigue of getting to know him
(R. Faesy, personal communication, August 9, 2005).

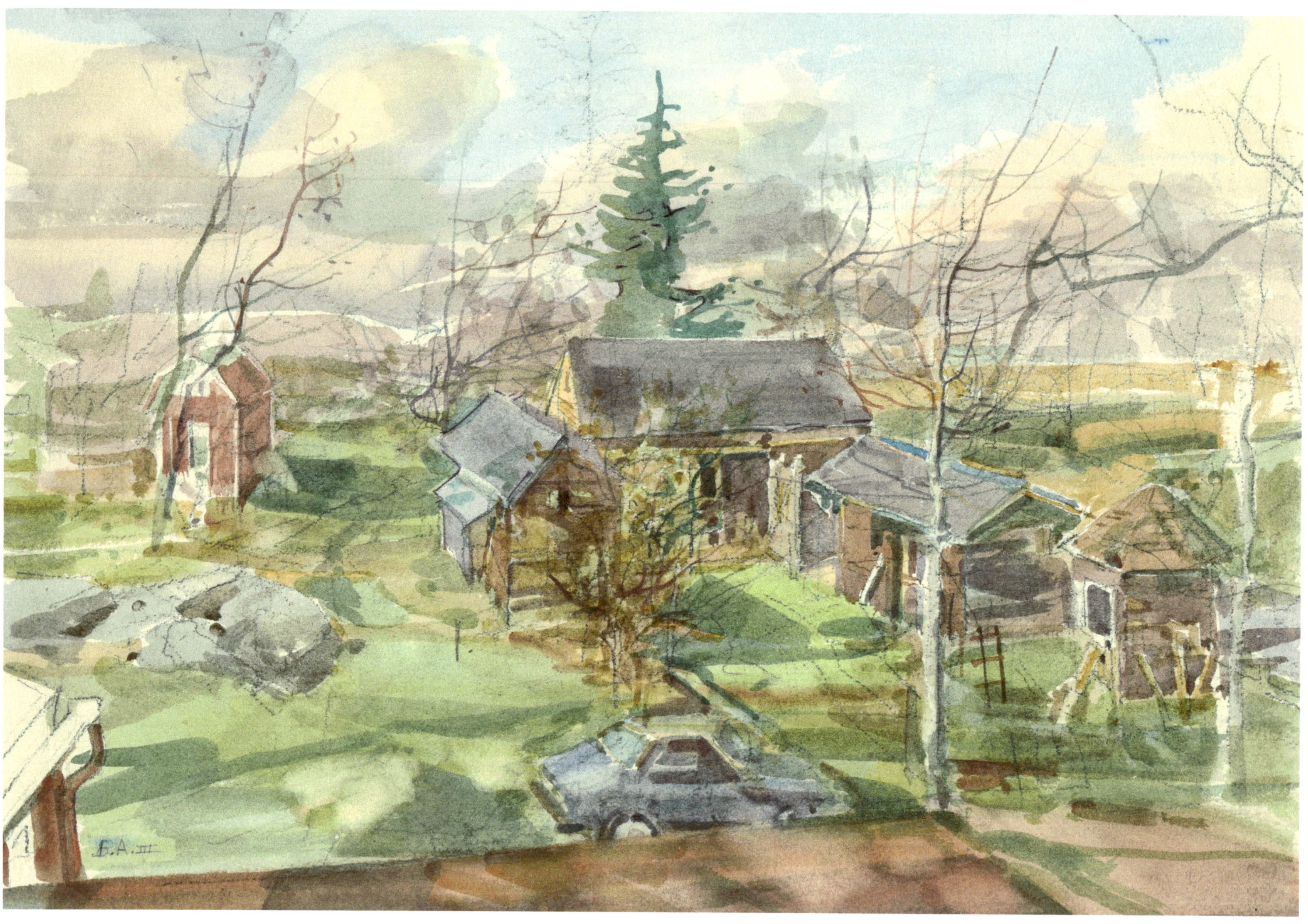

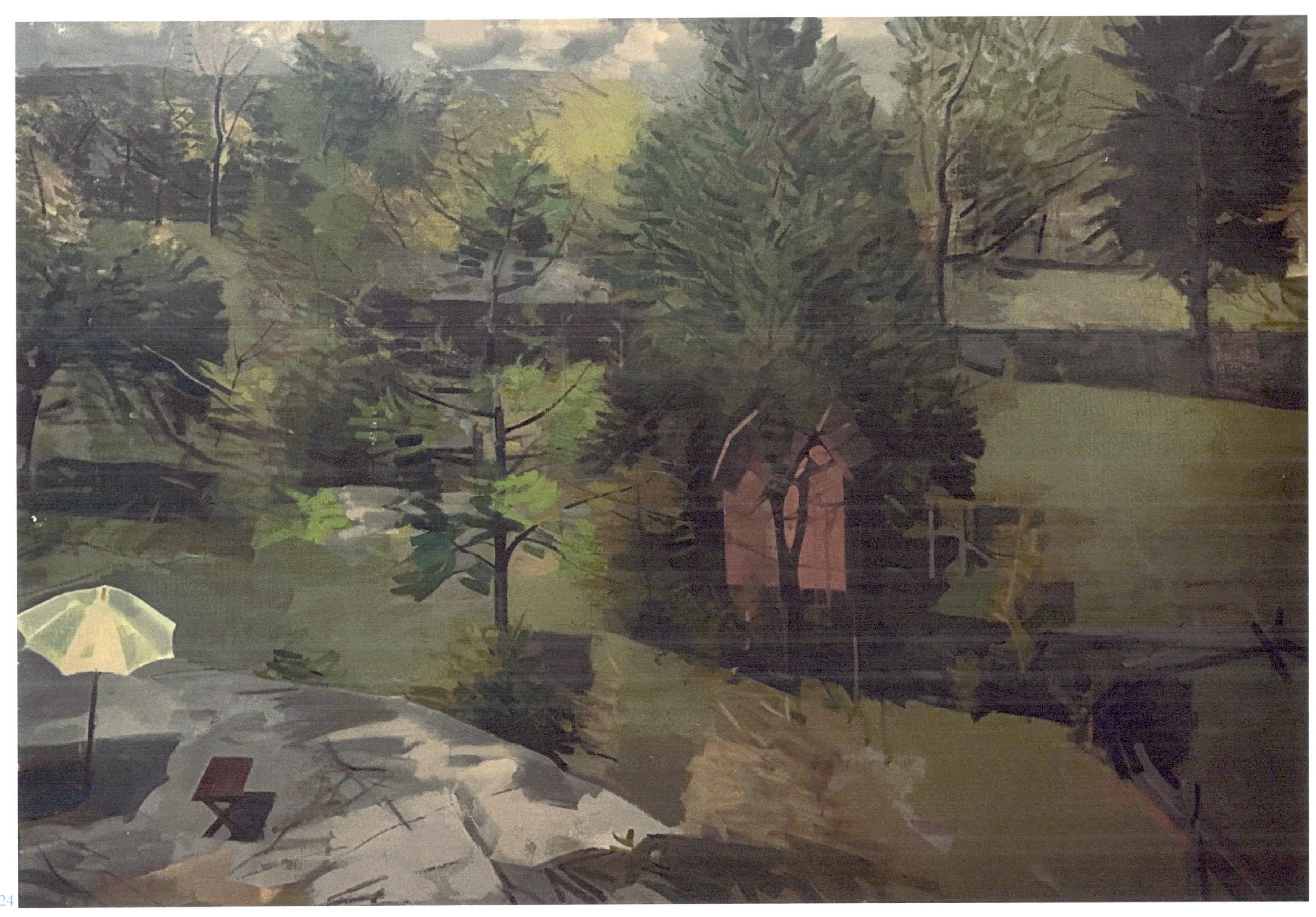

24

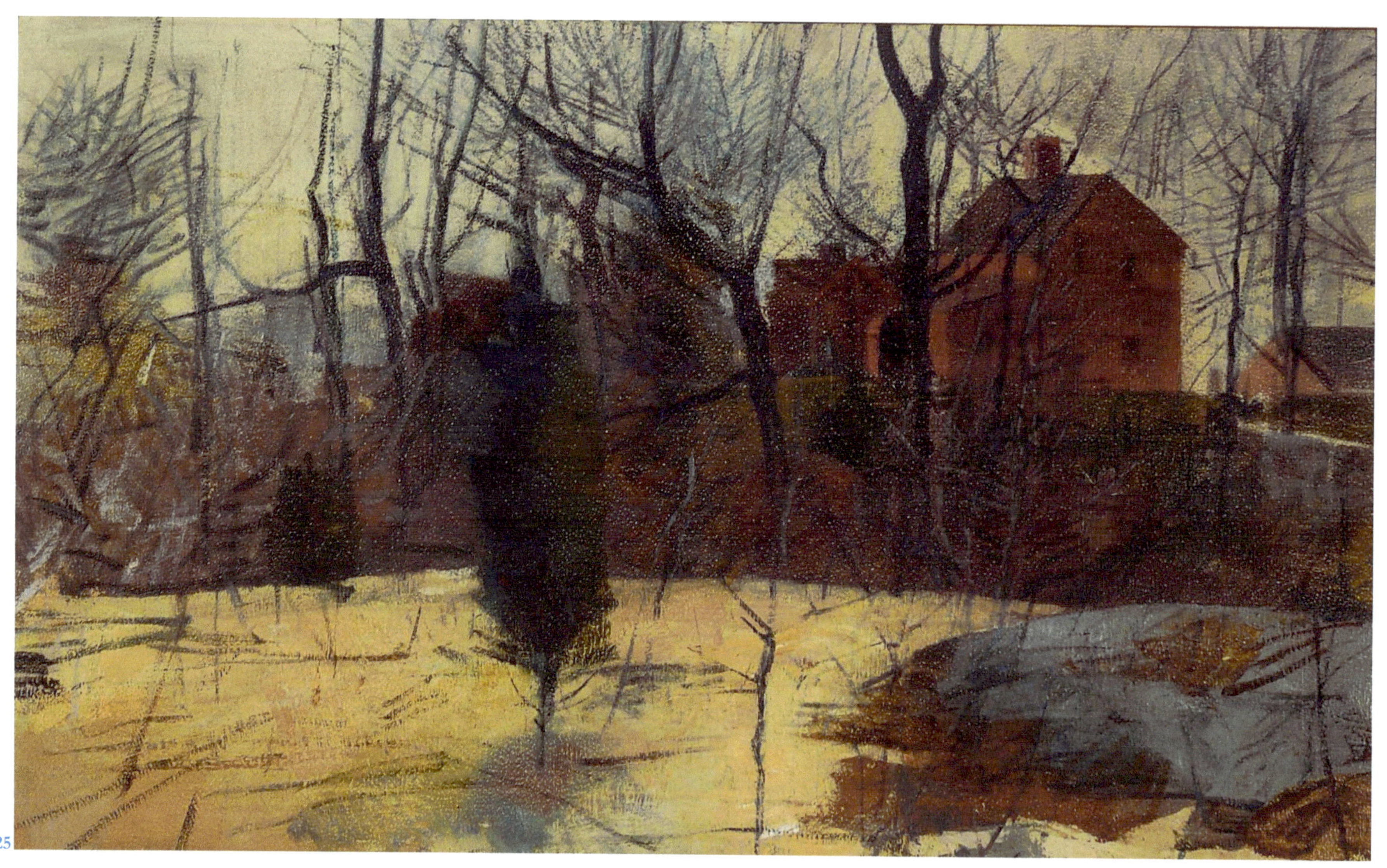

Sperry particularly liked the stony field across the road. One day he suffered a near-disaster there. He'd set up his easel and was at work on a painting when he became hungry and returned to the house for lunch. On returning to his easel, he found that one of Mr. Gully's cows had licked off most of the paint and, while depressed about that, he was frightened that the cow might be poisoned and die. Fortunately, it didn't (John Hubbard, personal communication, August 2005).

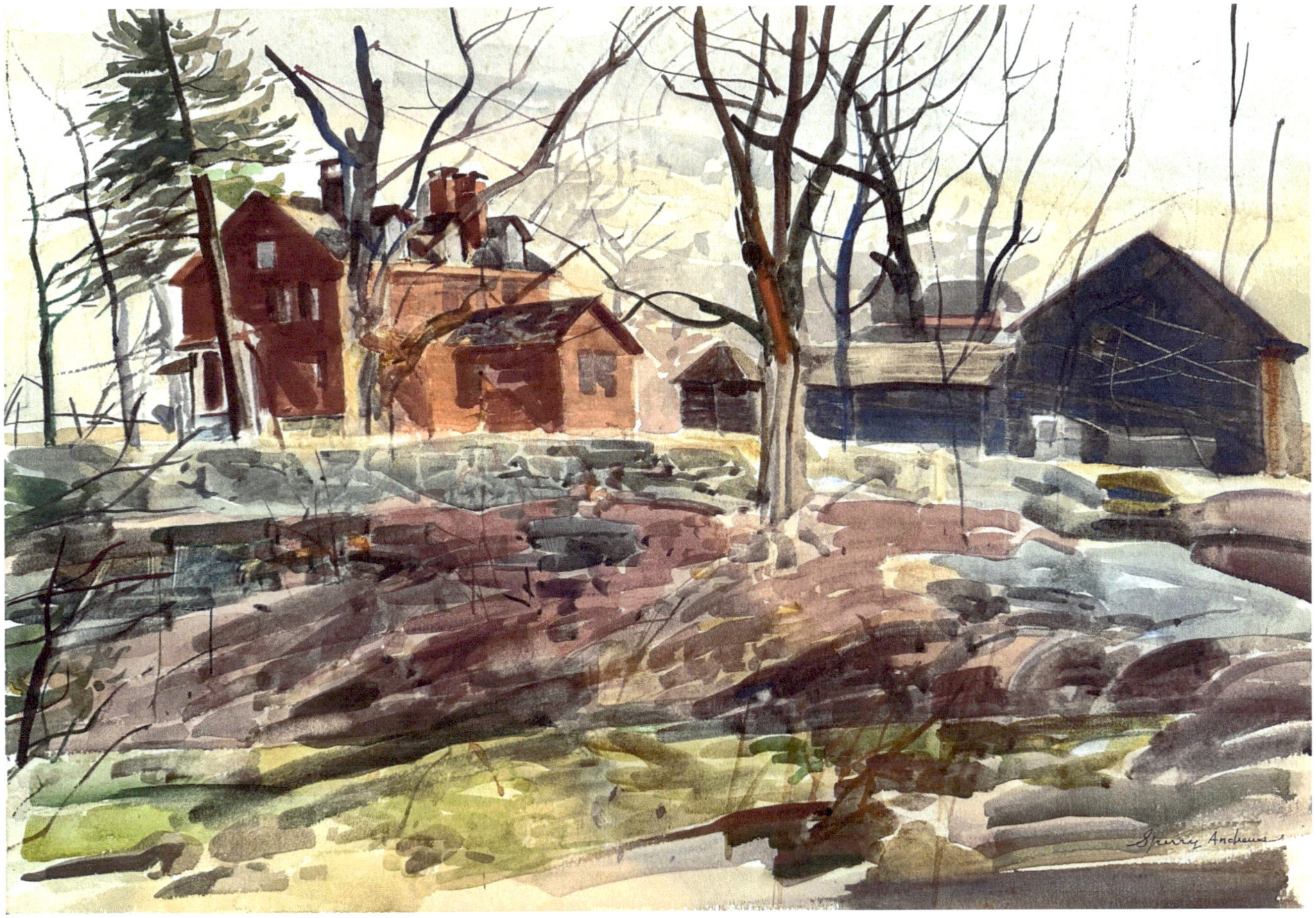

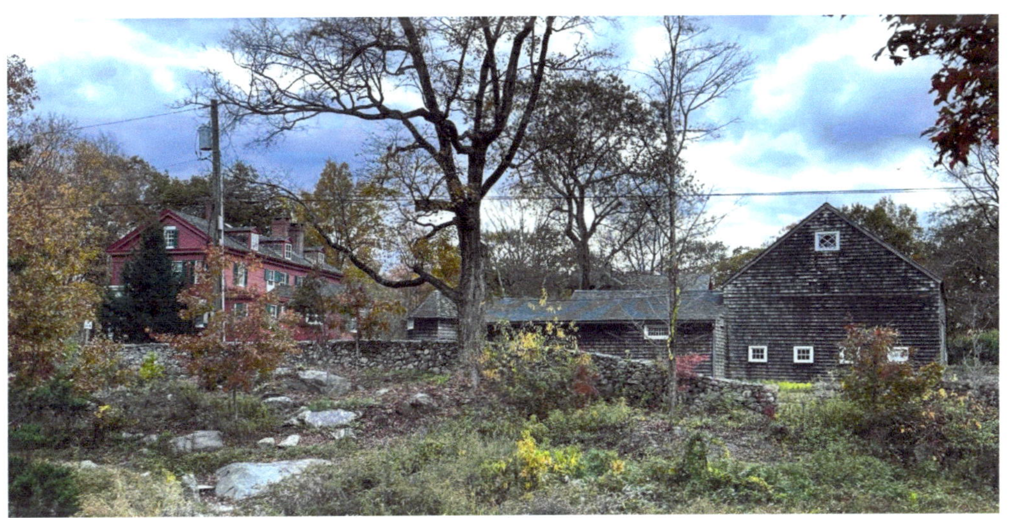

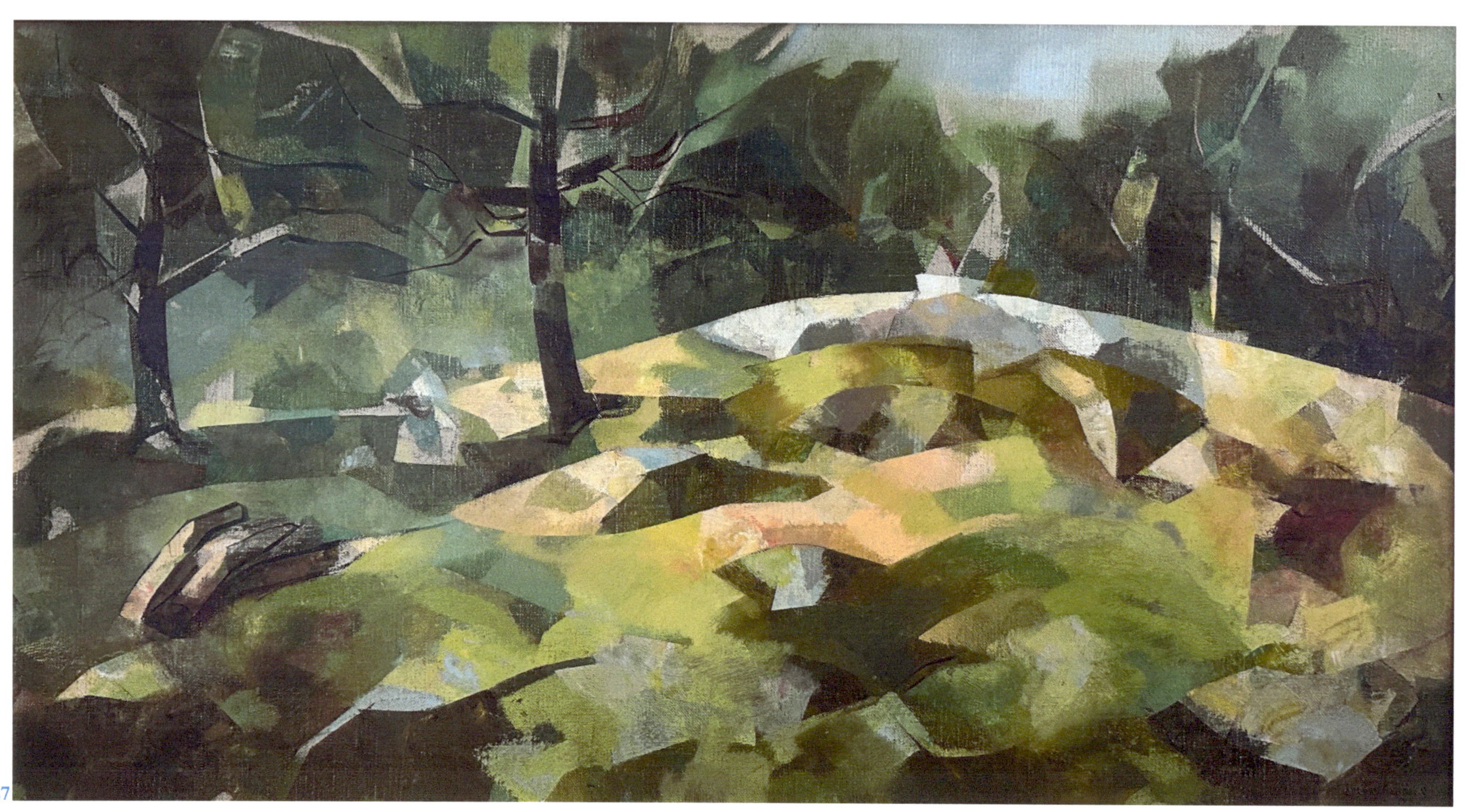

His sensitive drawings, forceful gouaches and monotypes evoke his Art Students League experience and lonely sojourn during military service in the barrens of Iceland, which awakened a sense of awe at the majesty of nature for him. His post-war explorations of Cézanne's example and Cubism are refined and miracles and not very well known. And finally, his three-plus decades of mature work at Weir Farm and in the New England landscape he knew and loved so well. (M. Chabot, eulogy, 2005)

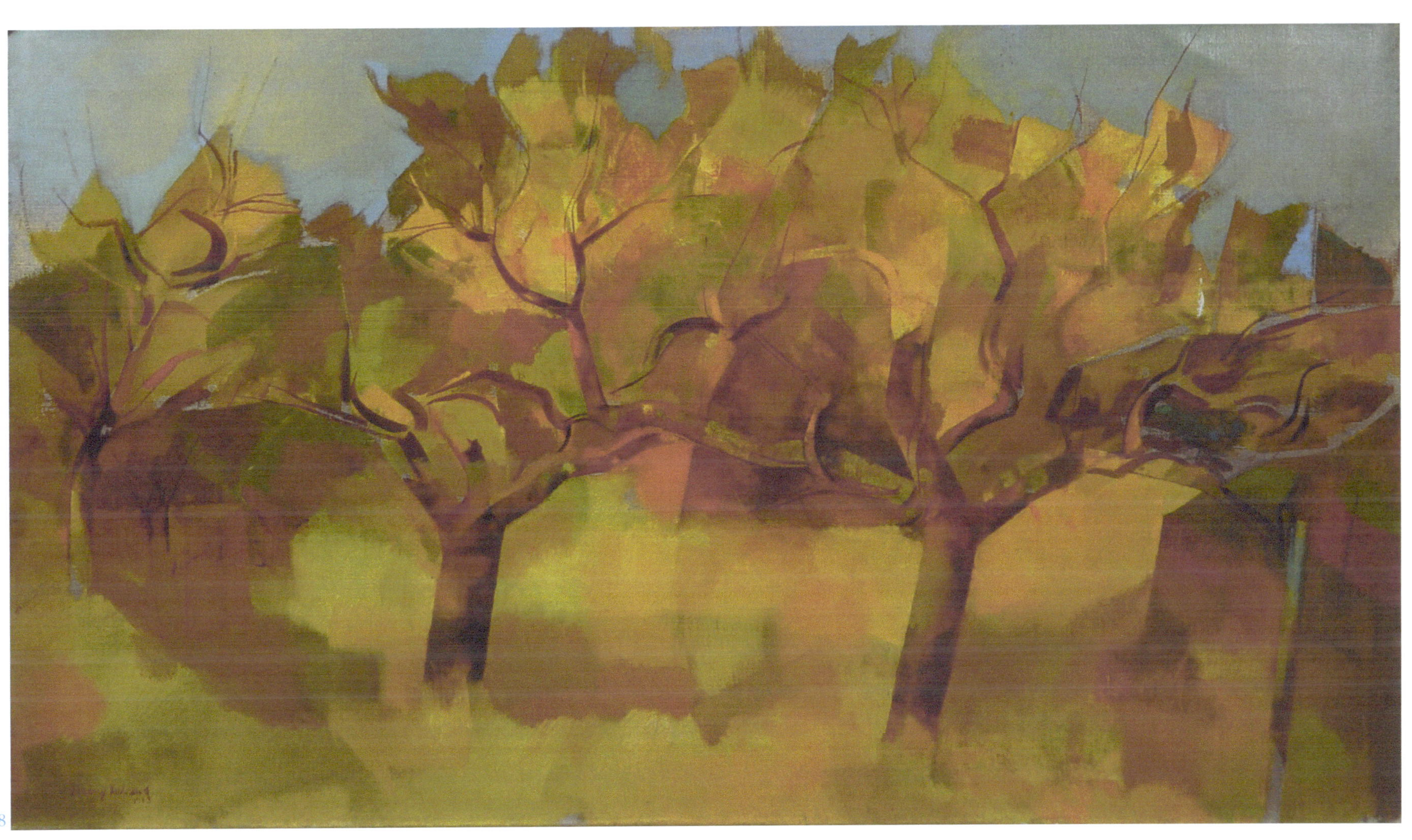

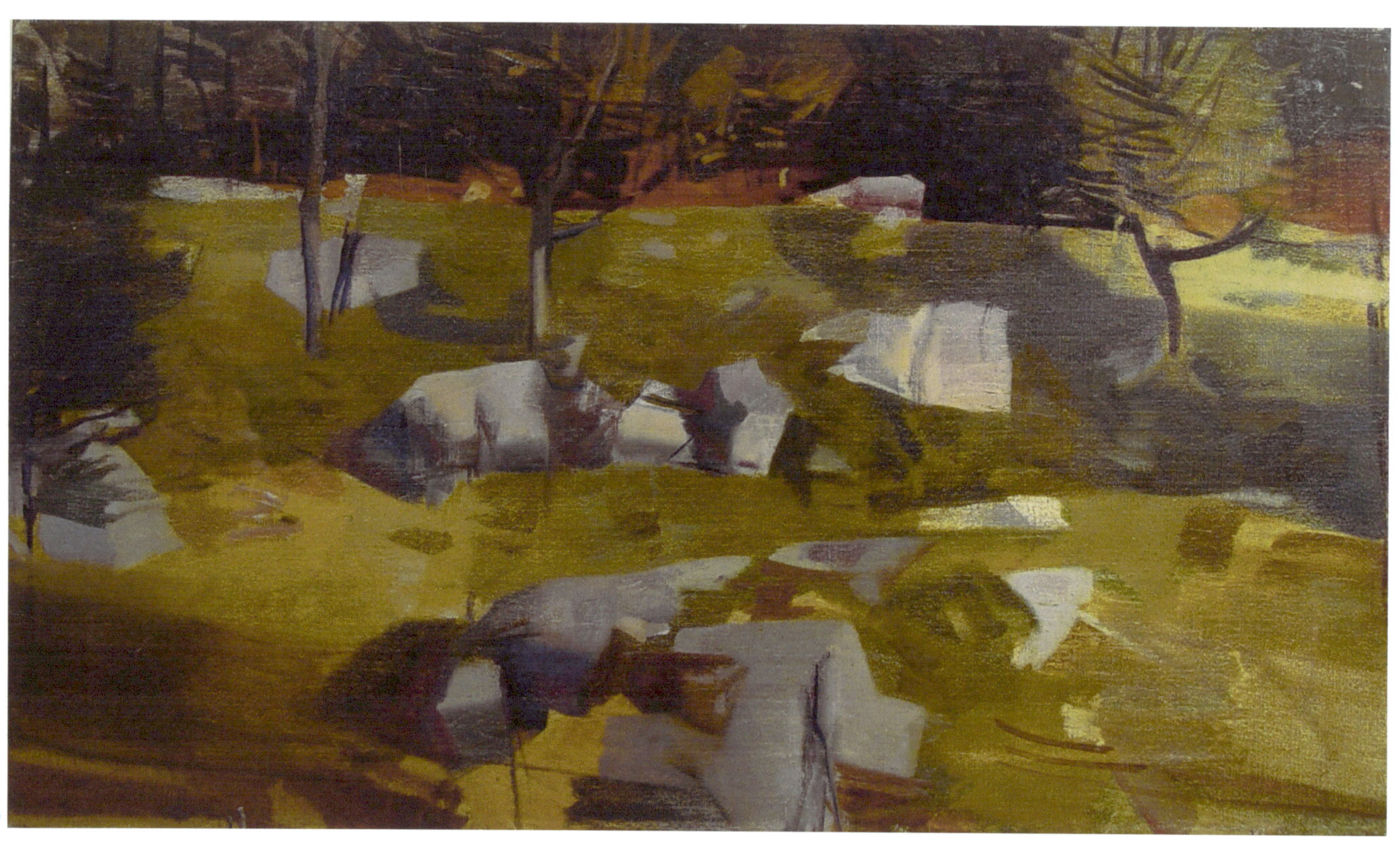

29

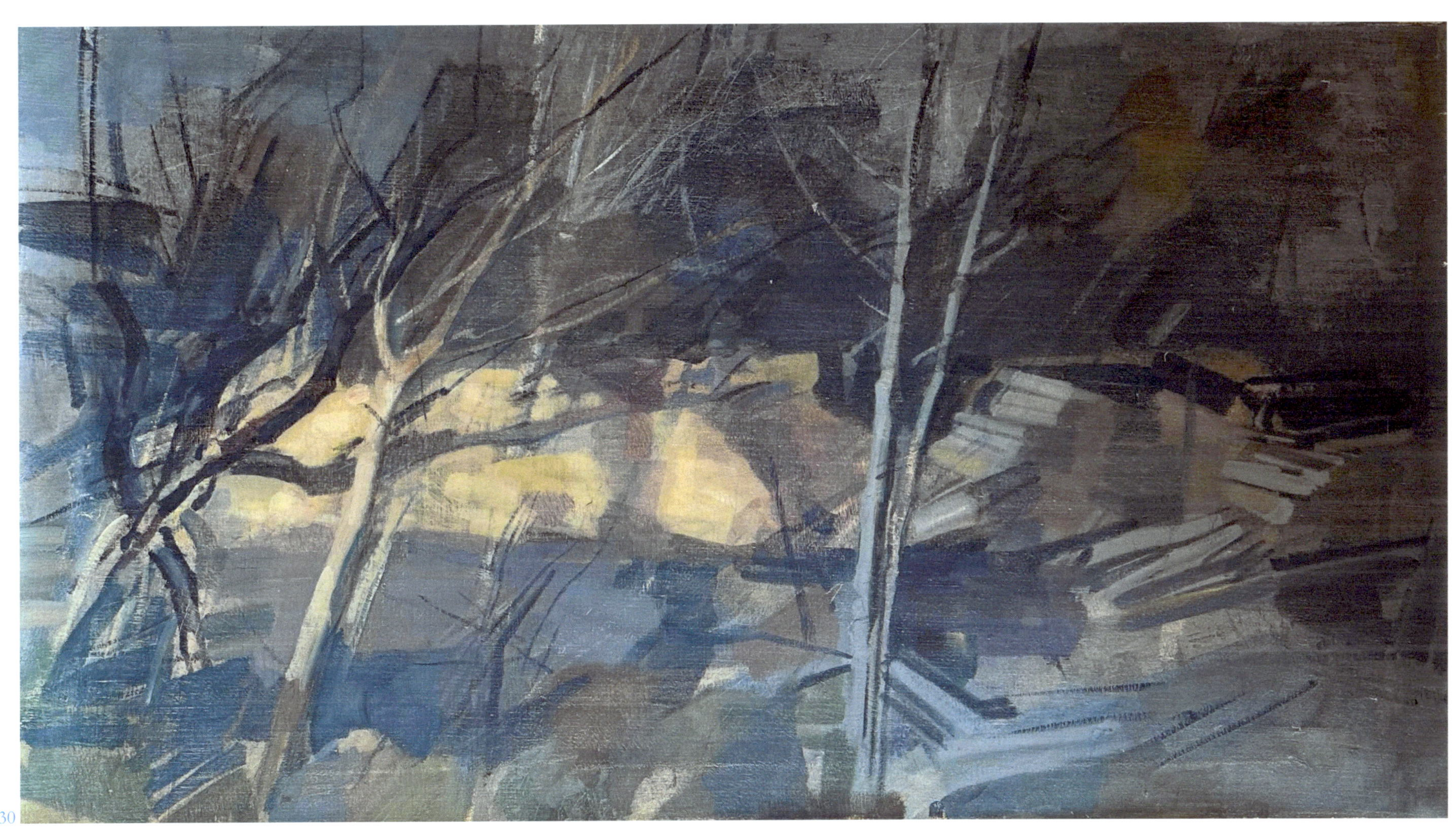

30

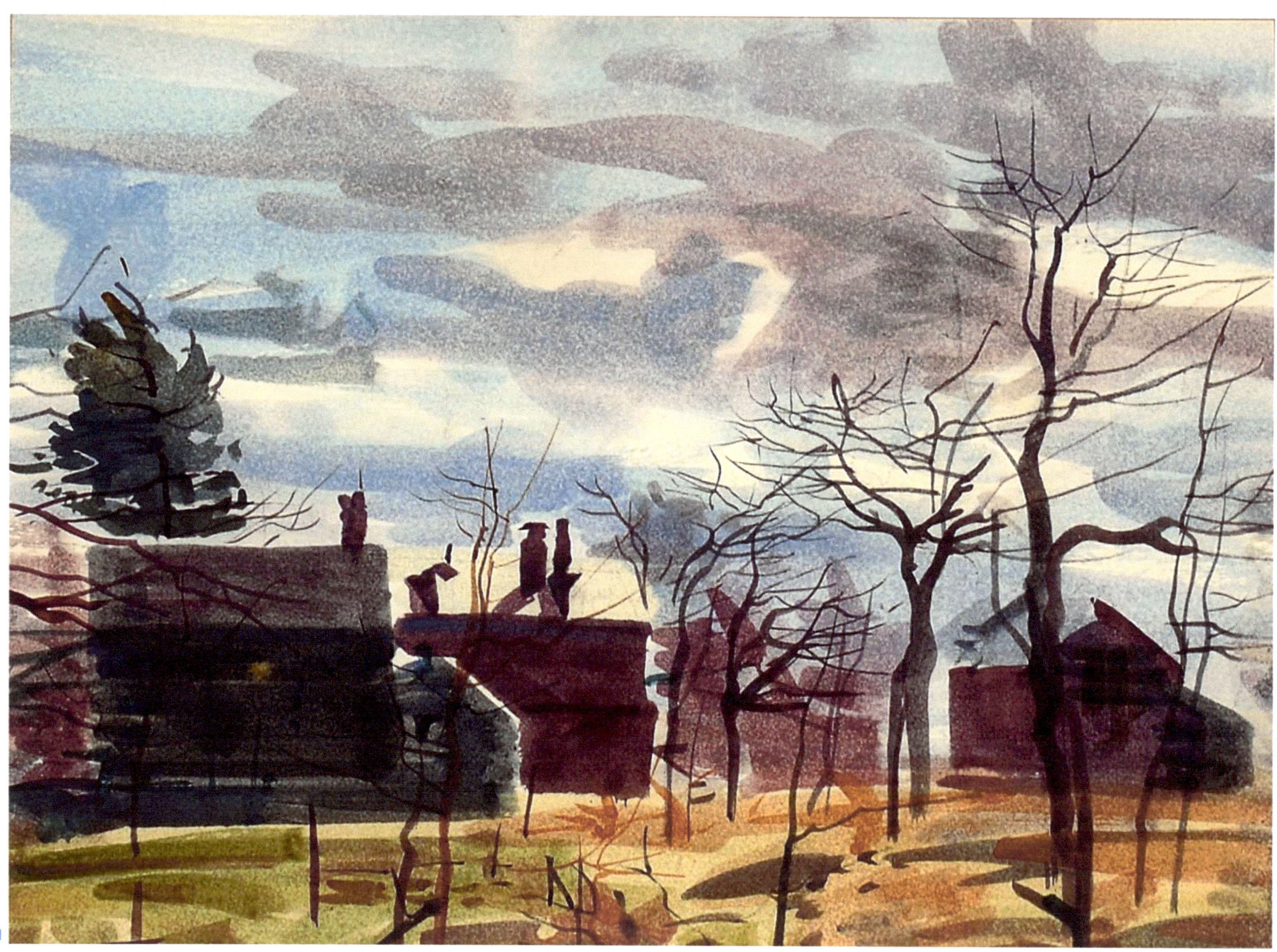

Dear Son:

It is a rainy Monday afternoon here at home. It has snowed at times and then back to rain again, a typical December performance. Your Dad failed to write to you last week. I will mail this letter this afternoon with the hope that it will reach you a few days before the holidays.

The news: The new roof is completed and it looks beautiful, you should see it on a bright day it has a warm gold look to it. The new copper flashings on the chimney gleam and the repaired skylight over the attic stairway is also copper framed now.

I have walked to the cemetery several times to admire the new roof from there. The scaffolding etc. for the job still on the place to be picked up.

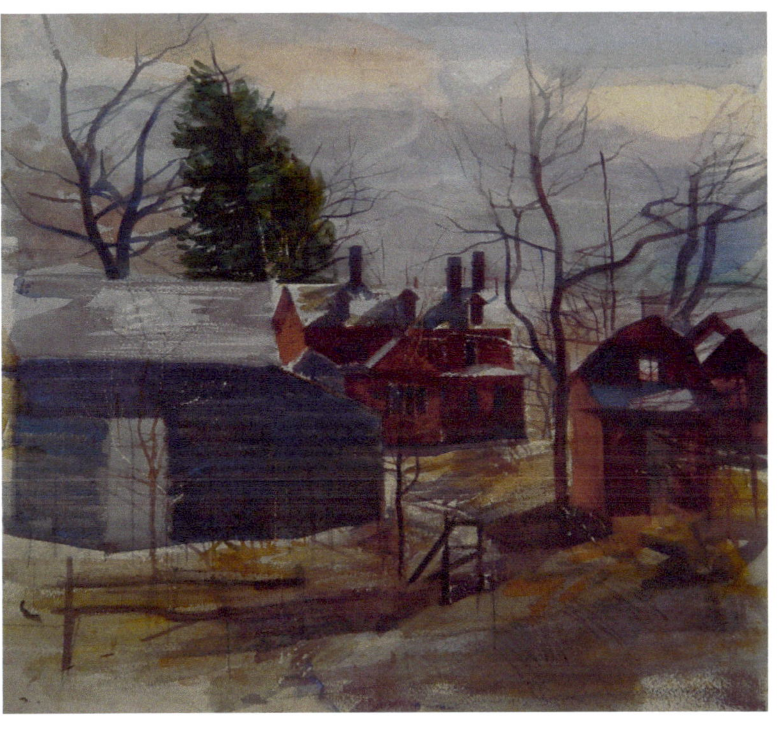

32

Dear Son:
It is a rainy Monday afternoon here at home. It has snowed at times and then back to rain again, a typical December performance. The new roof is completed and it looks beautiful; you should see it on a bright day. It has a warm gold look to it. The new copper flashings on the chimney gleam and the squared skylight over the stairway is also framed now. I have walked to the cemetery several times to admire the new roof from there. (Letter to the author, December 23, 1975)

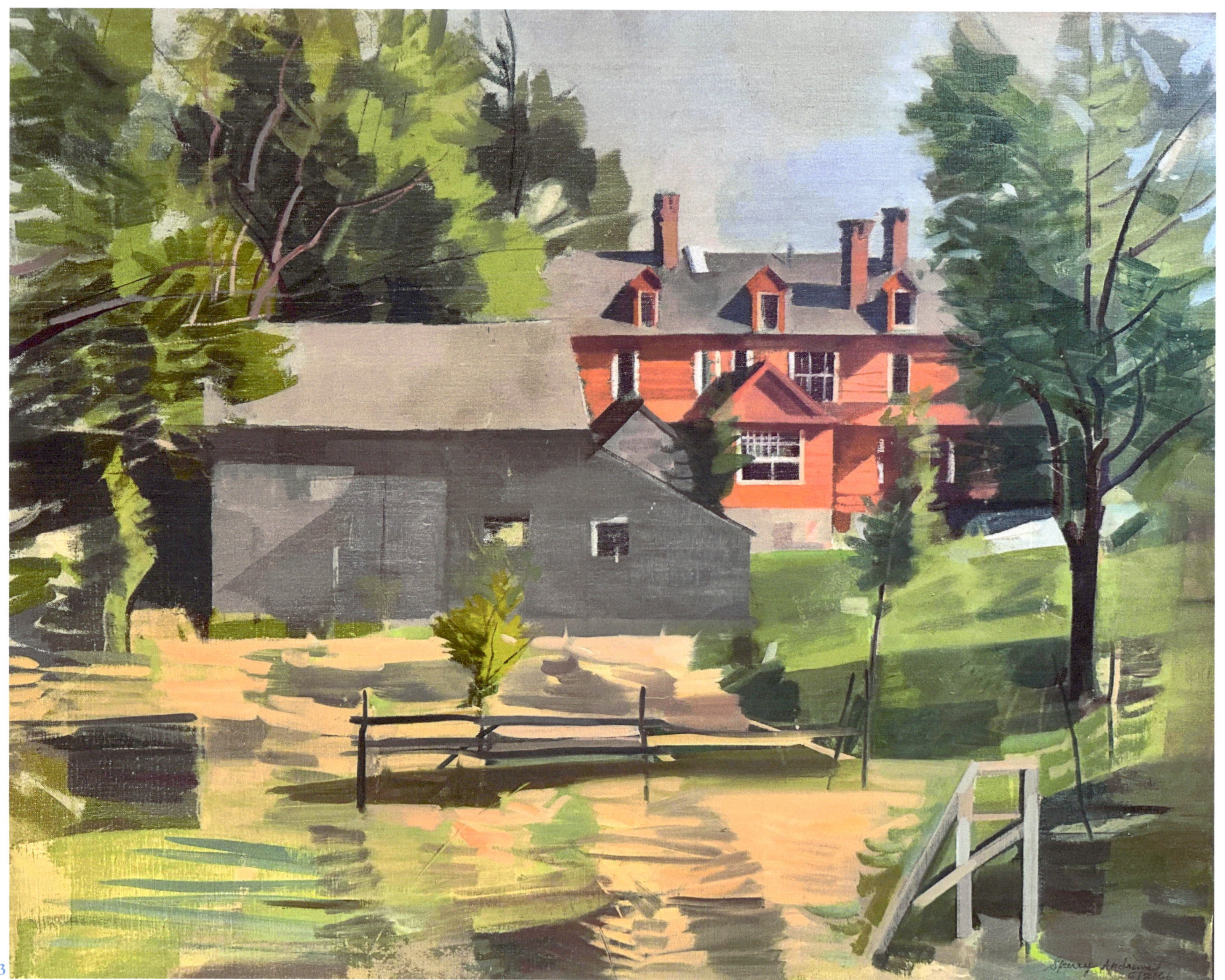

Sperry Andrews

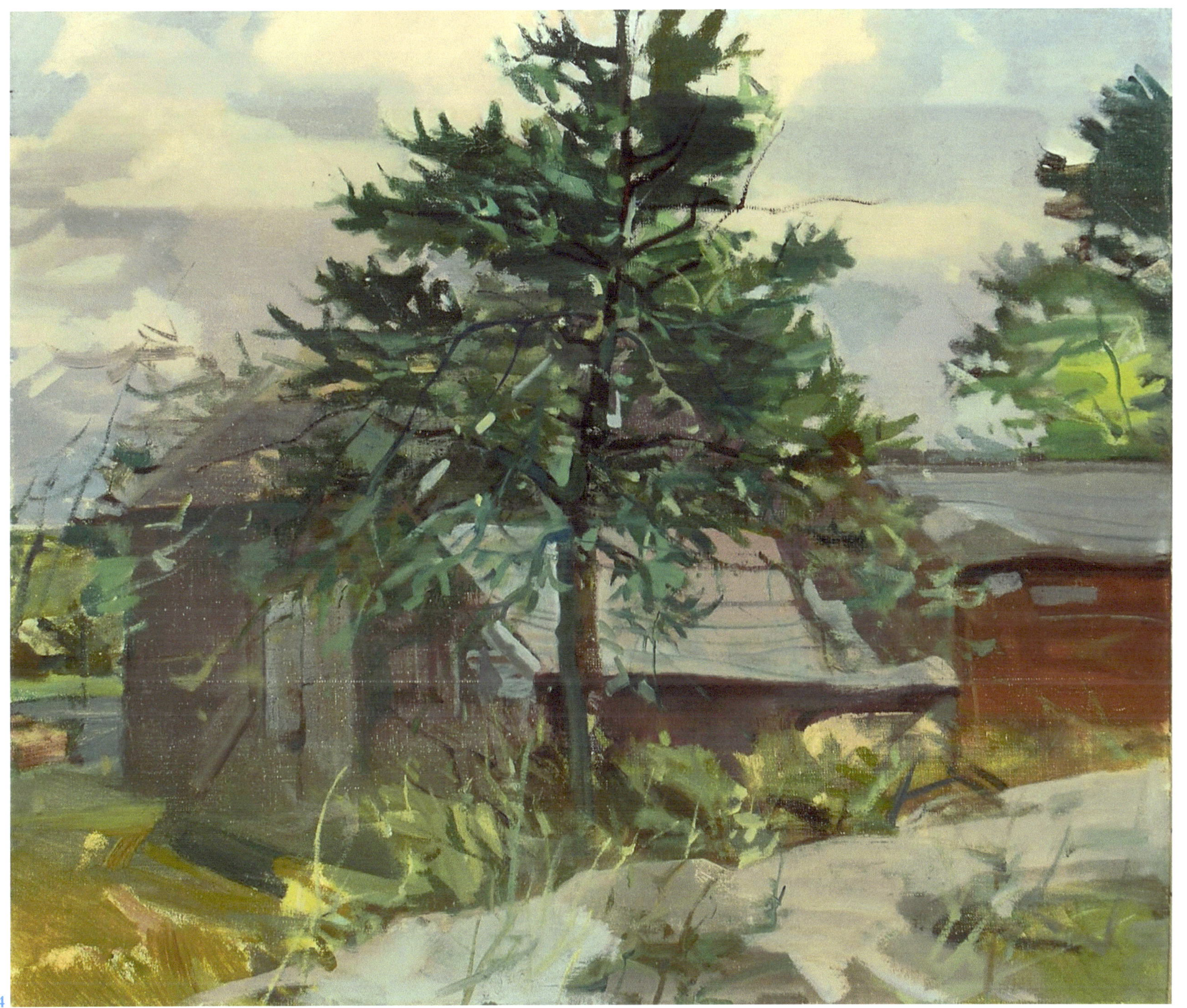

34

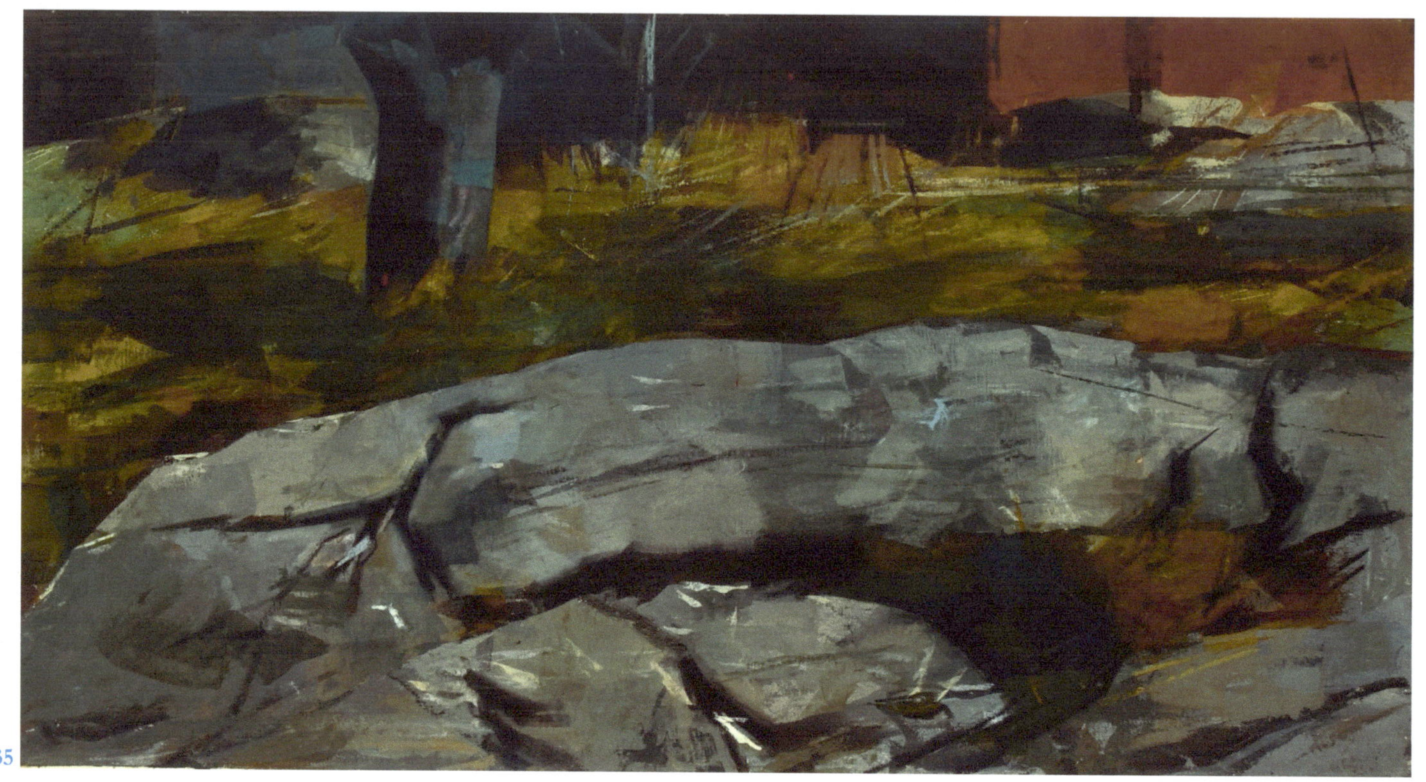

35

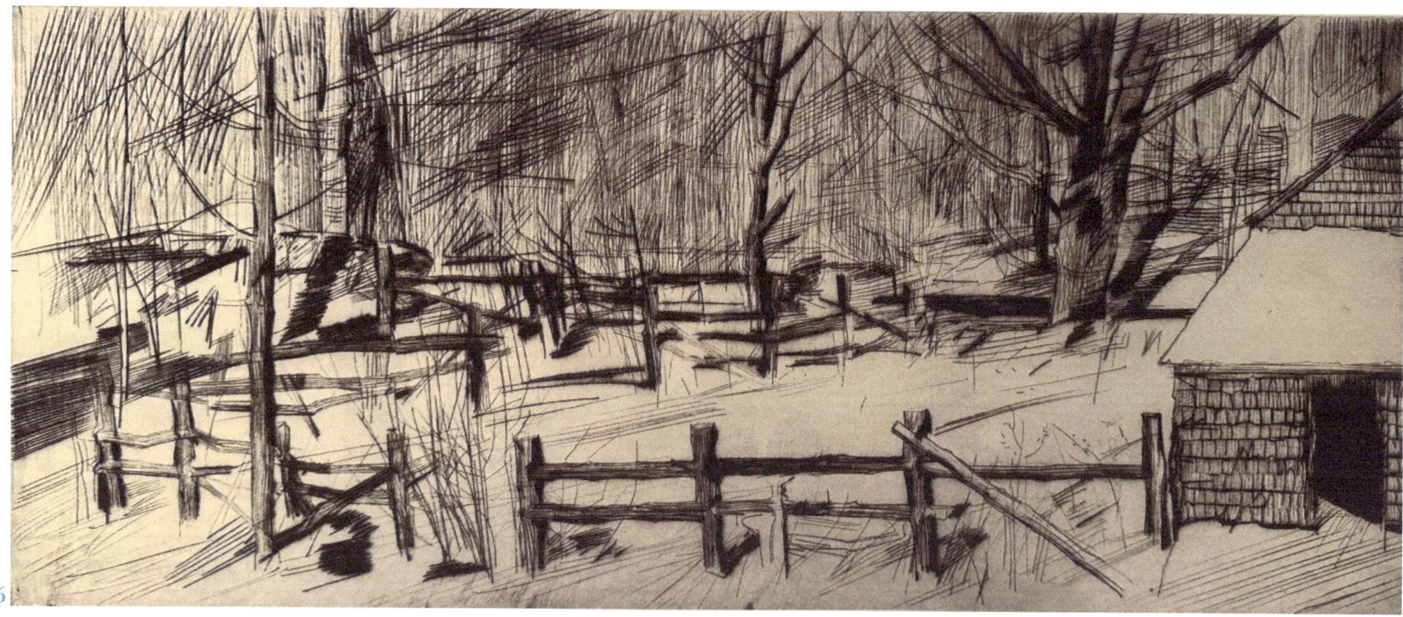

36

38

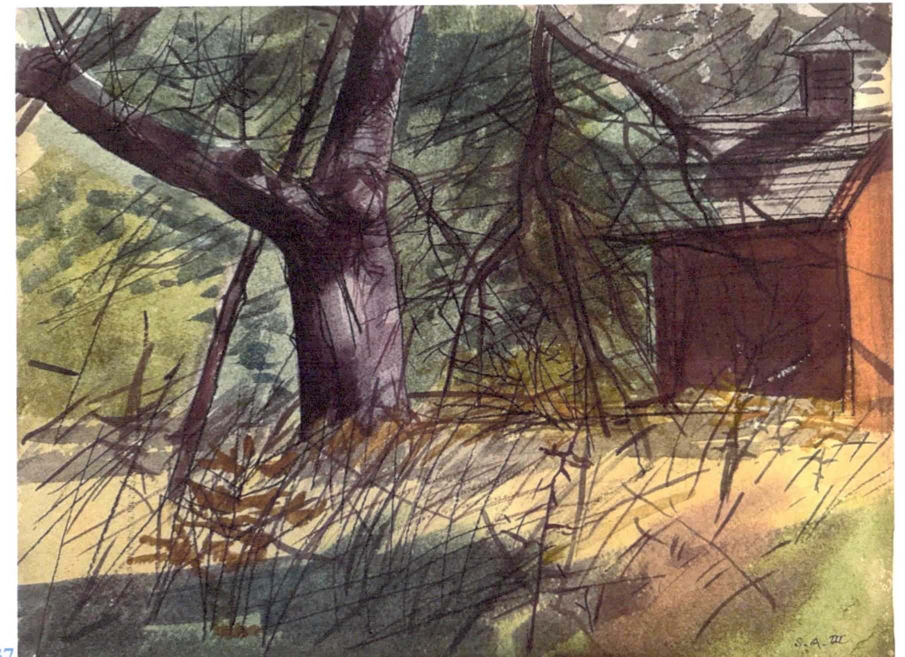

37

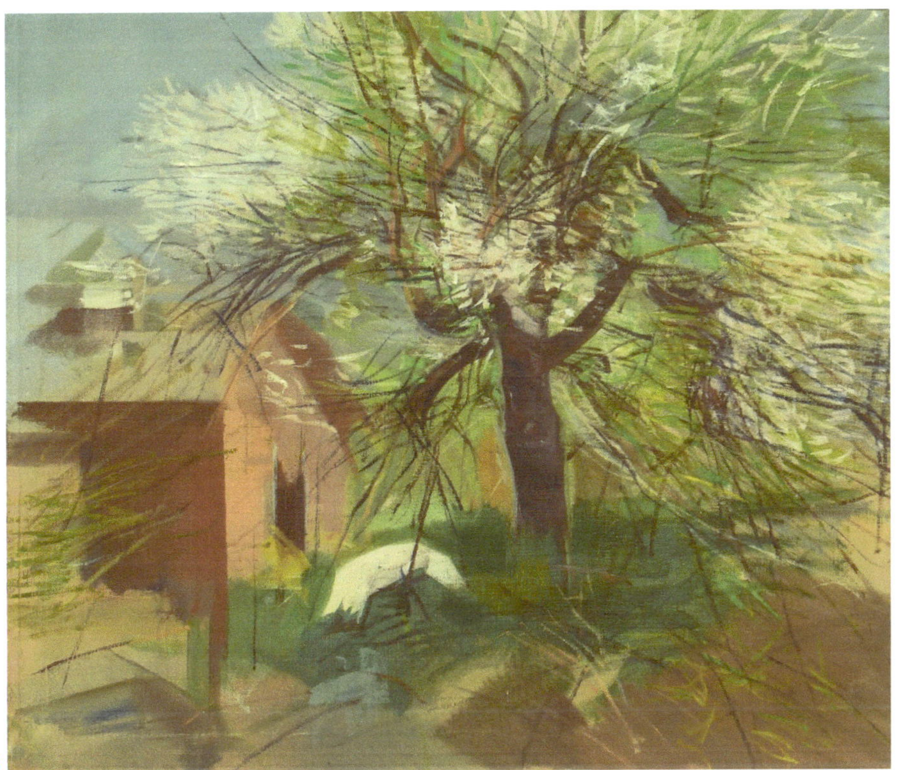

38

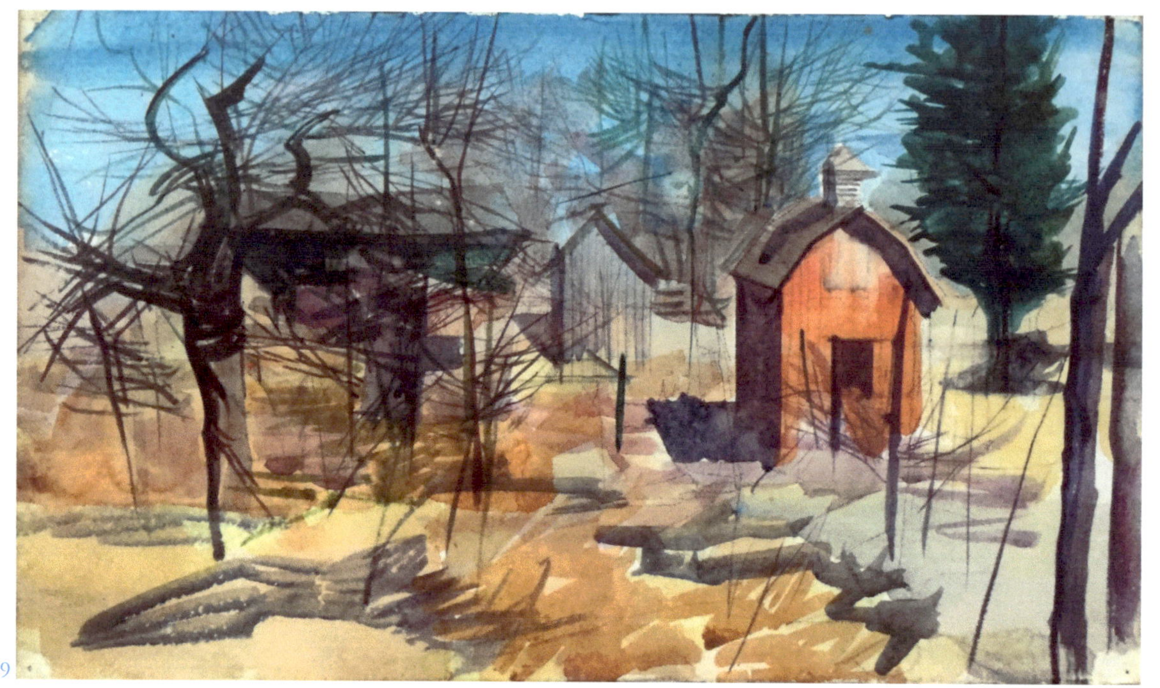

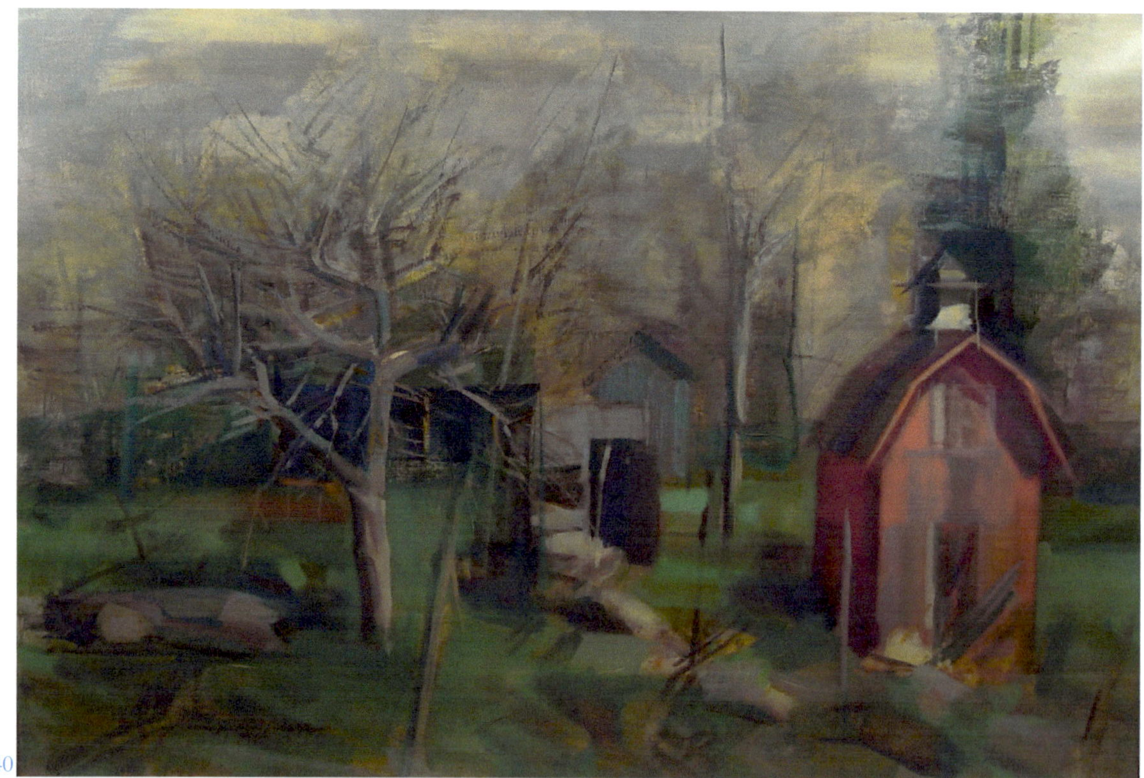

40

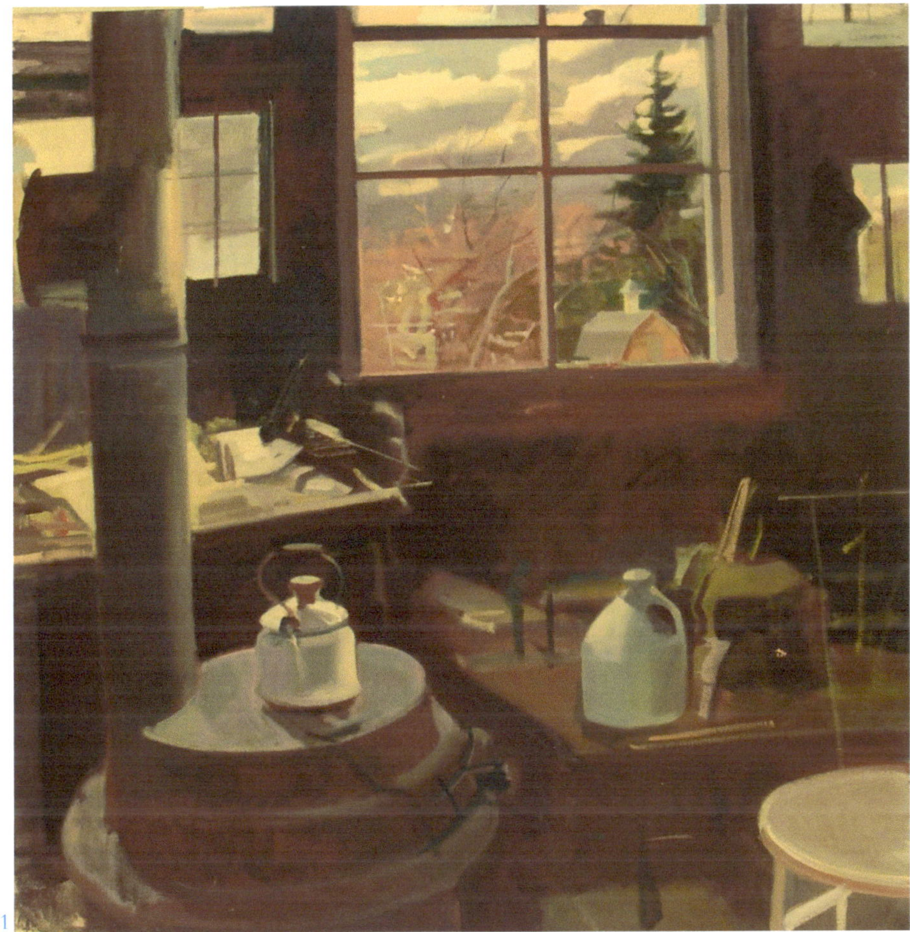 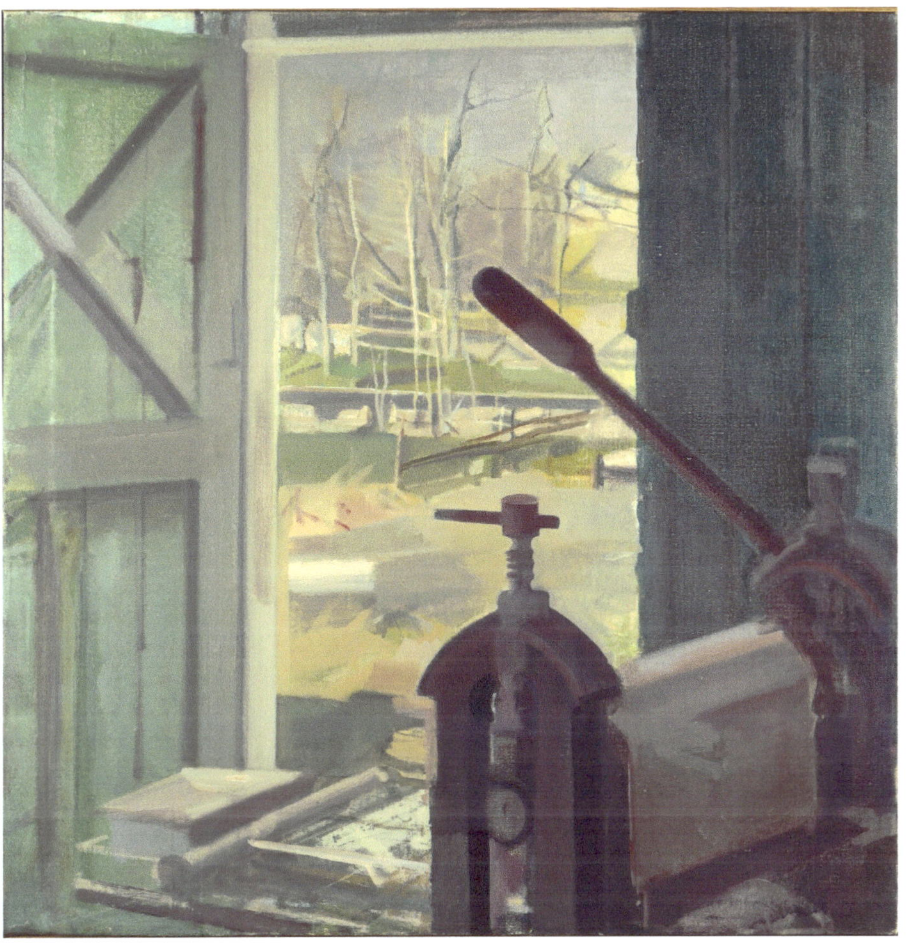

My father used the Weir studio year-round, especially in winter. He worked with the door open in summer. On Saturday he listened to the Texaco Metropolitan Opera broadcasts of Puccini, Bellini, Mozart, Verdi and Wagner. I recall him wondering if the latter was apt.

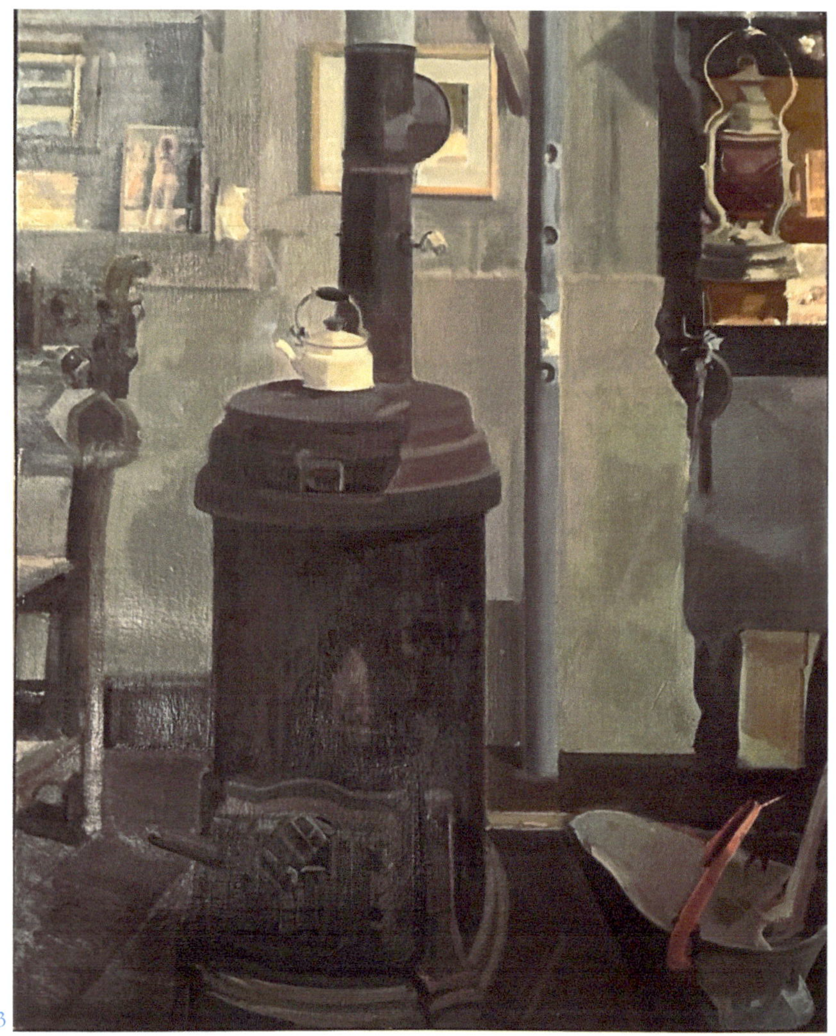 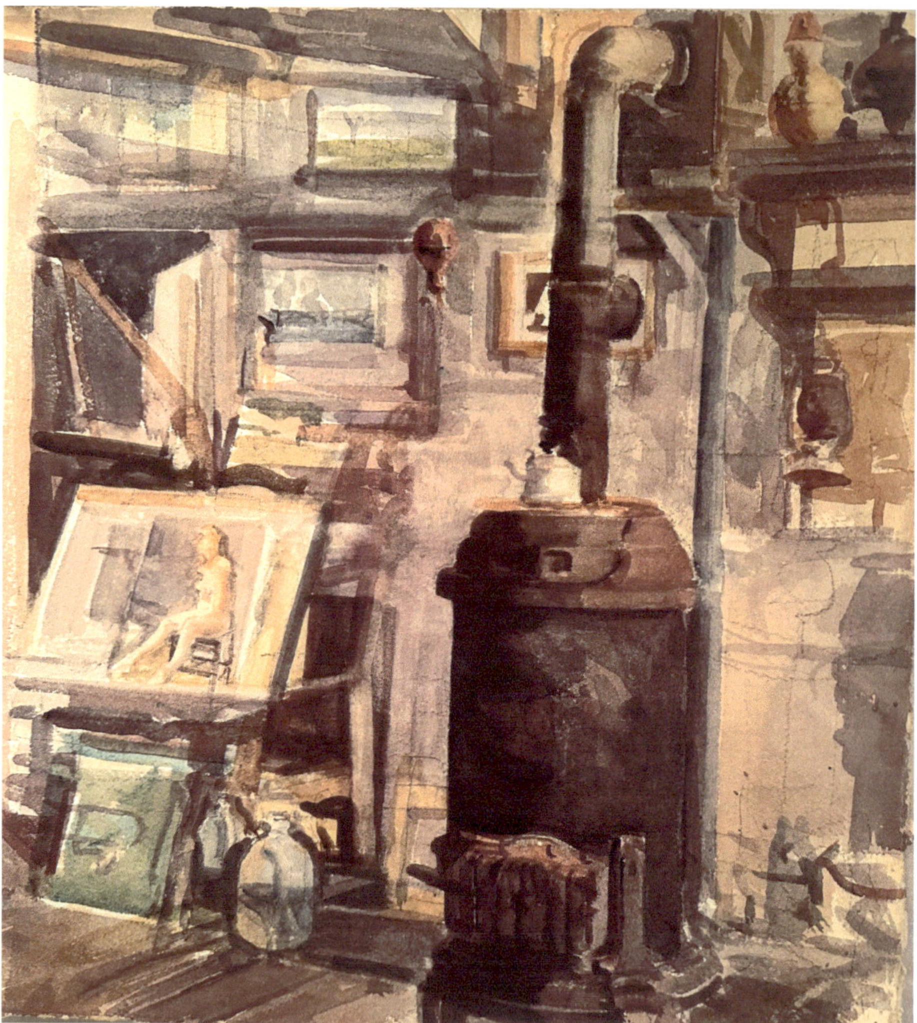

A Friday evening at home, during the daylight hours, time was spent working on a painting — the subject, my warm morning space heater (stove) in the small studio. This particular canvas has been a prop for more than a year; perhaps I should have abandoned it months ago? Tonight, looking at it under the fluorescent light, it looks overworked, a look I know all too well. Better to begin with a fresh eye and forget the old effort. (Letter to the editor February 3, 1975)

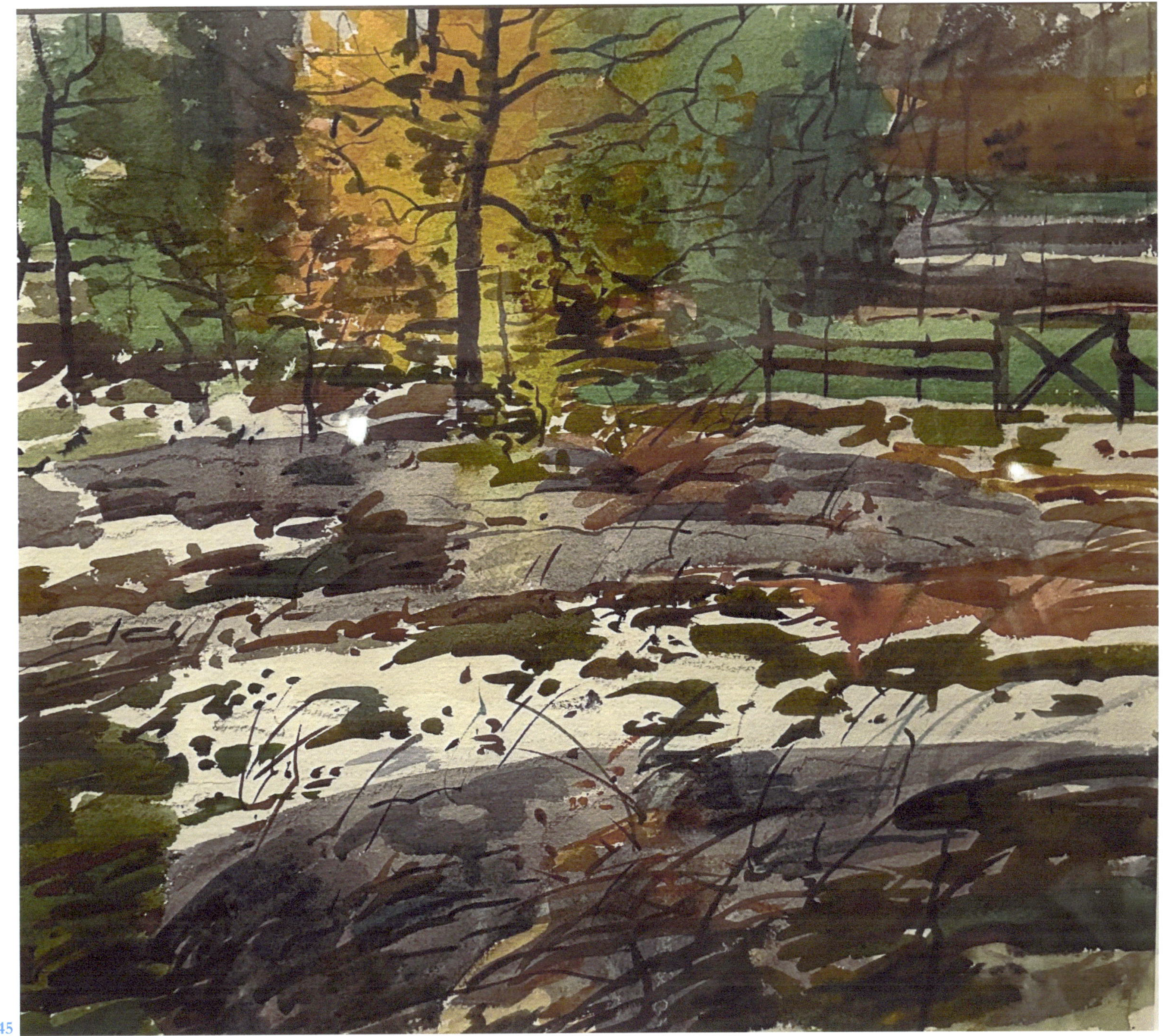

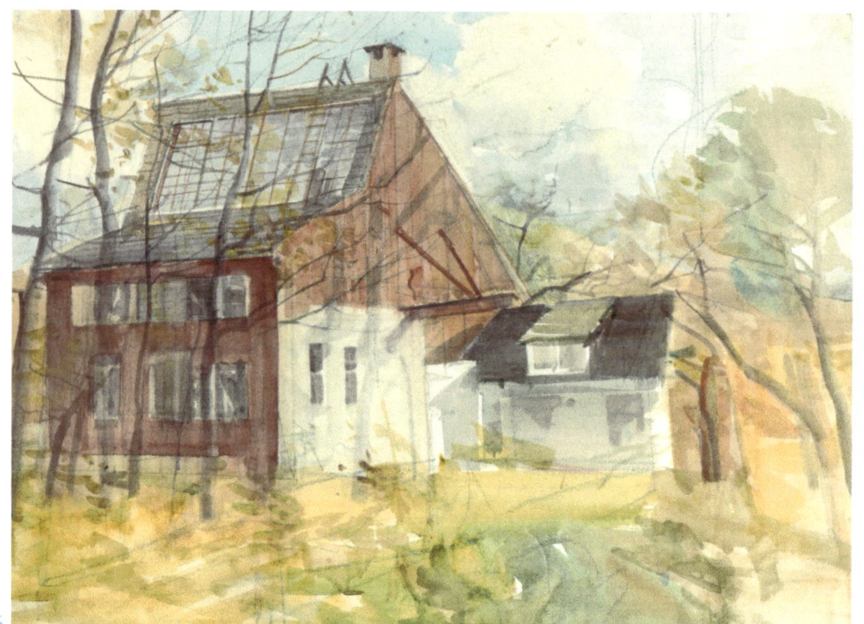

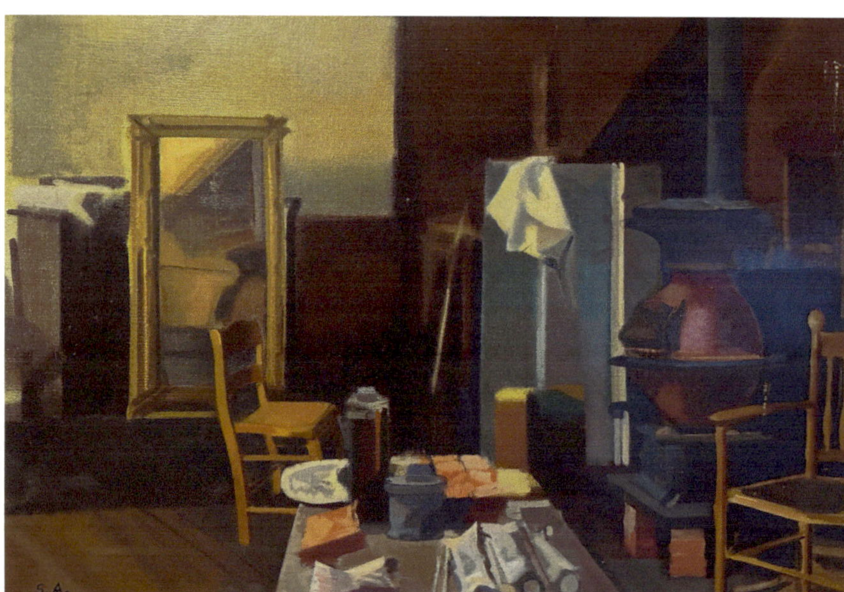

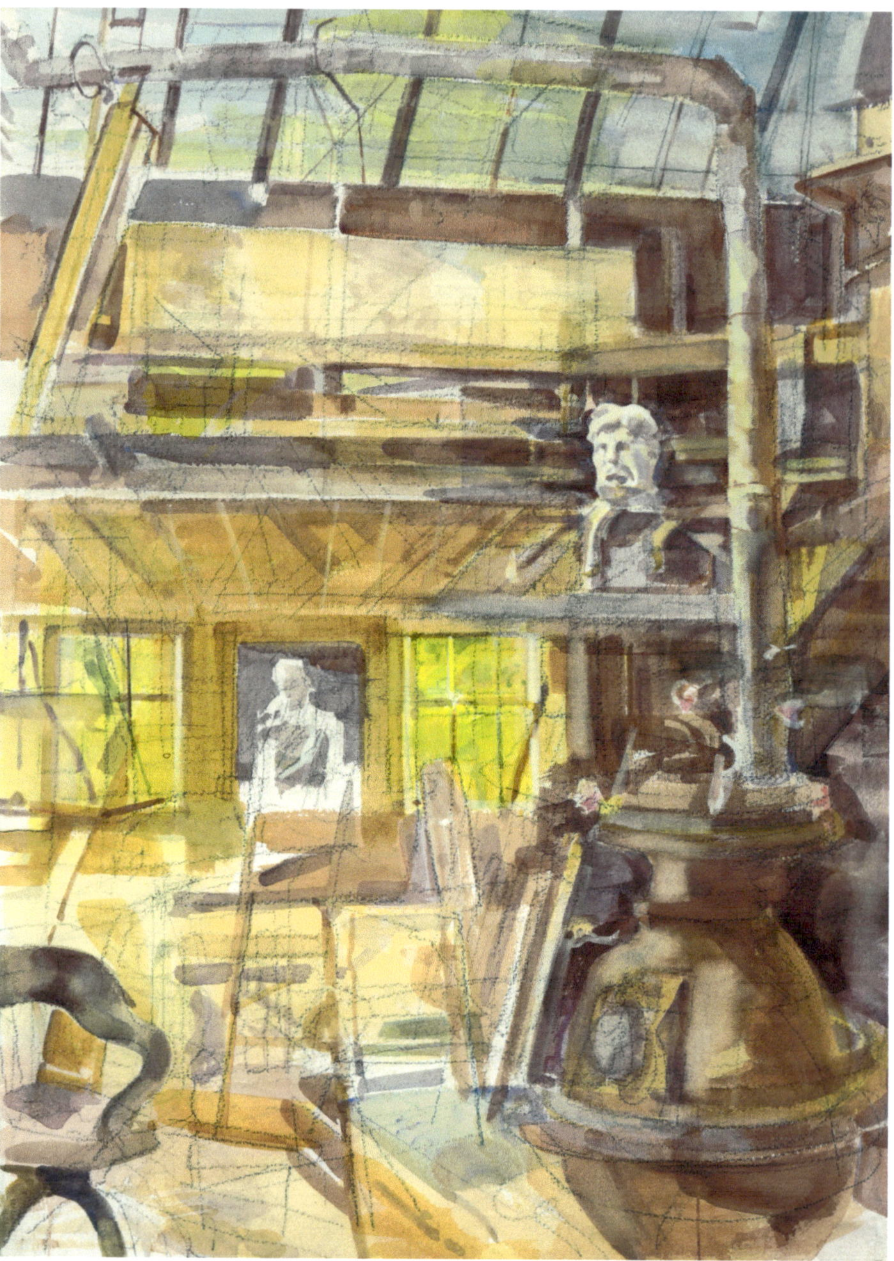

The big (Young) studio was used less in the winter because it took a long time to warm up. It was always used for life drawing and frequently for revising works that were begun en plein air. The interiors of both studios were the subjects of numerous still lifes.

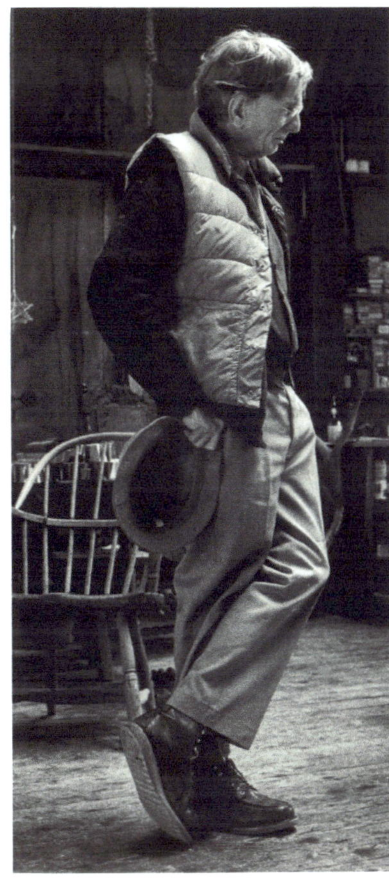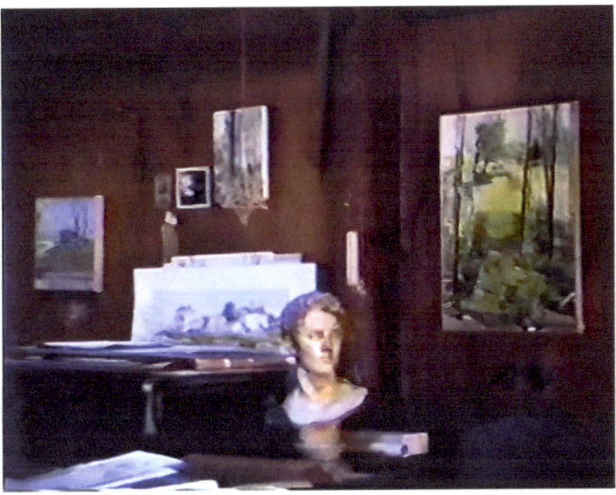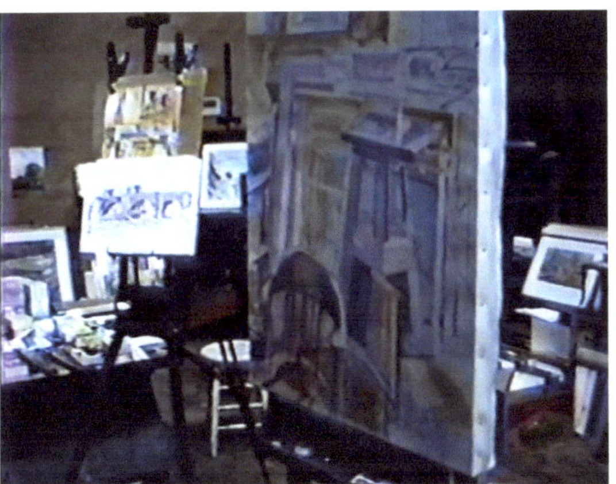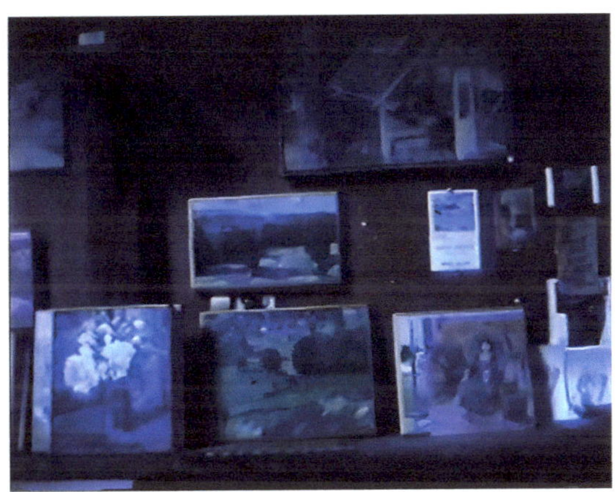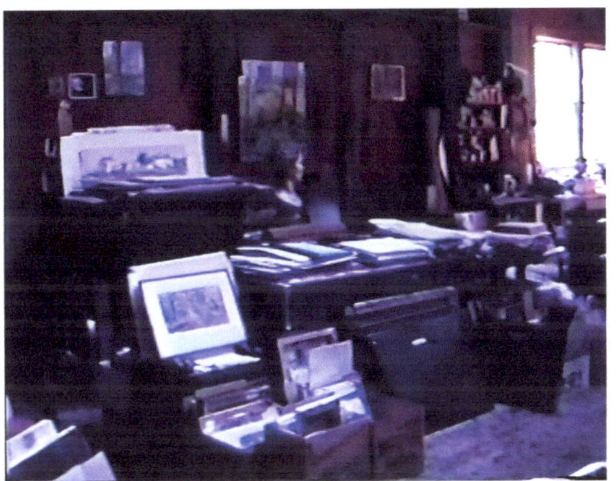

Everywhere one looked, there were beautiful oils, watercolors and drawings by Mr. Andrews on the walls, easels, in deep stacks, racks and piles against the walls and on every flat surface. Here in layer upon layer was an artist's fine and full life. I spent an ecstatic afternoon carefully going through stacks of stretched and unstretched oils, watercolors, drawings, scratch boards, pastels, monotypes and even a few etchings. I was amazed at the lively vitality of his drawings, the often surgical precision with which he observed and rendered man-made and natural form alike. His watercolors were a revelation with their fluid execution and ability to capture fleeting light and color in the ever-changing landscape. His oils confirmed his masterful draftsmanship as well, his sense of composition and unique color, but something more. I began to see early works which showed Sperry's youthful intellectual and artistic ferment and reveal aspects of his inner emotional life. The full measure of Sperry's vast body of work slowly revealed itself in all its subjects, media, styles and moods. (M. Chabot, eulogy, 2005)

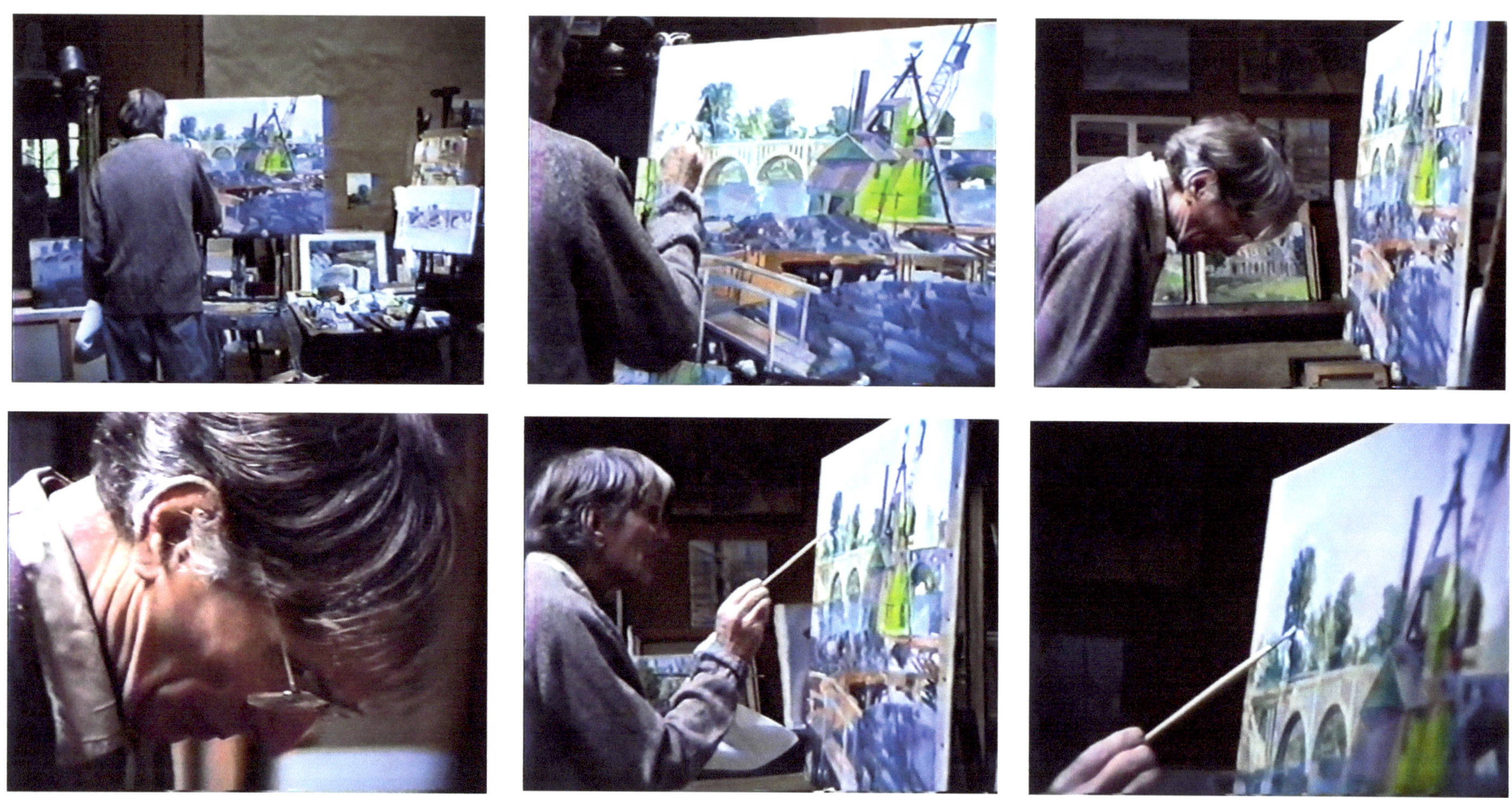

You must be completely organized within your reach, the essentials. Don't lose time fussing about locating colors, brushes etc. It will take numerous bad days to have a fairly successful time. I have experienced sometimes for no particular reasons a good day and then when one expects the ideal, which seldom does present itself one has a poor time (notes, May 9, 1977).

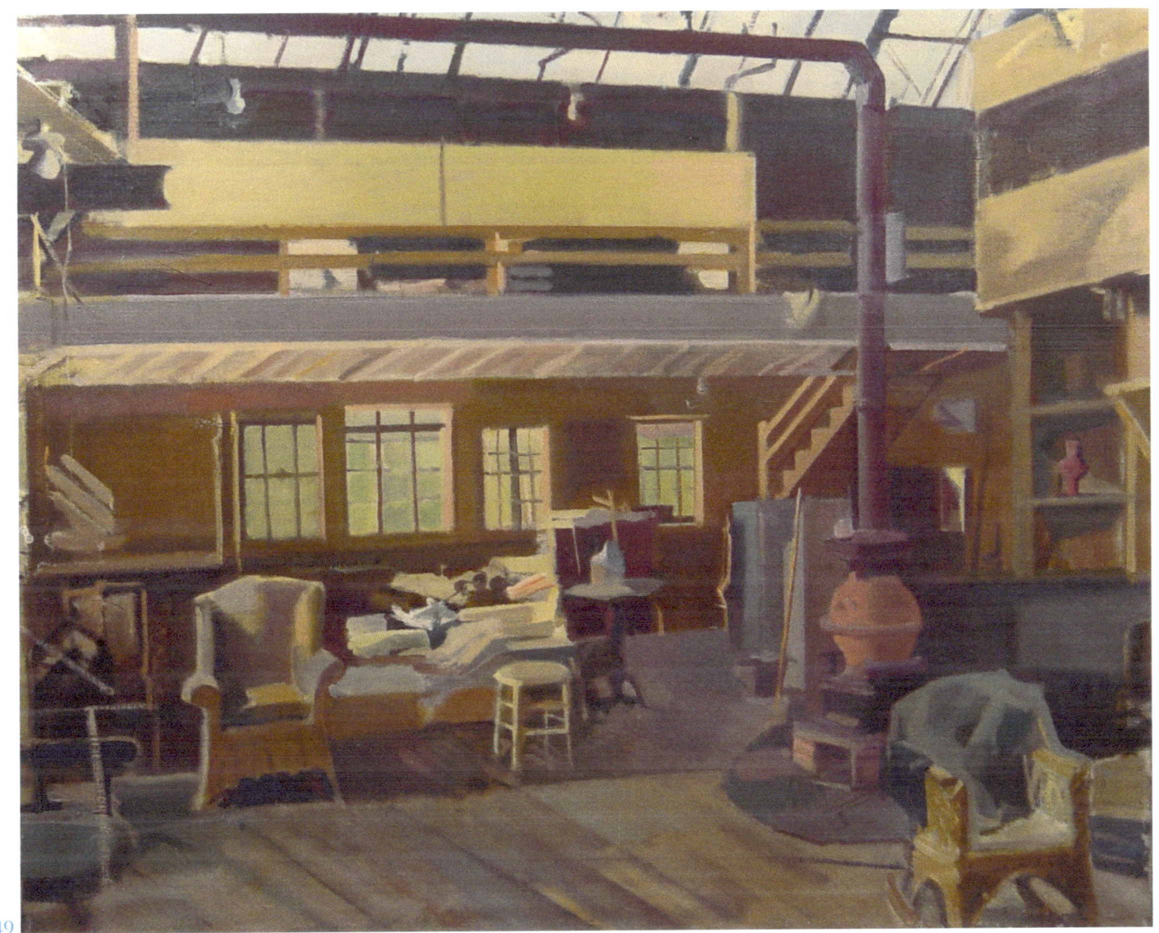

49

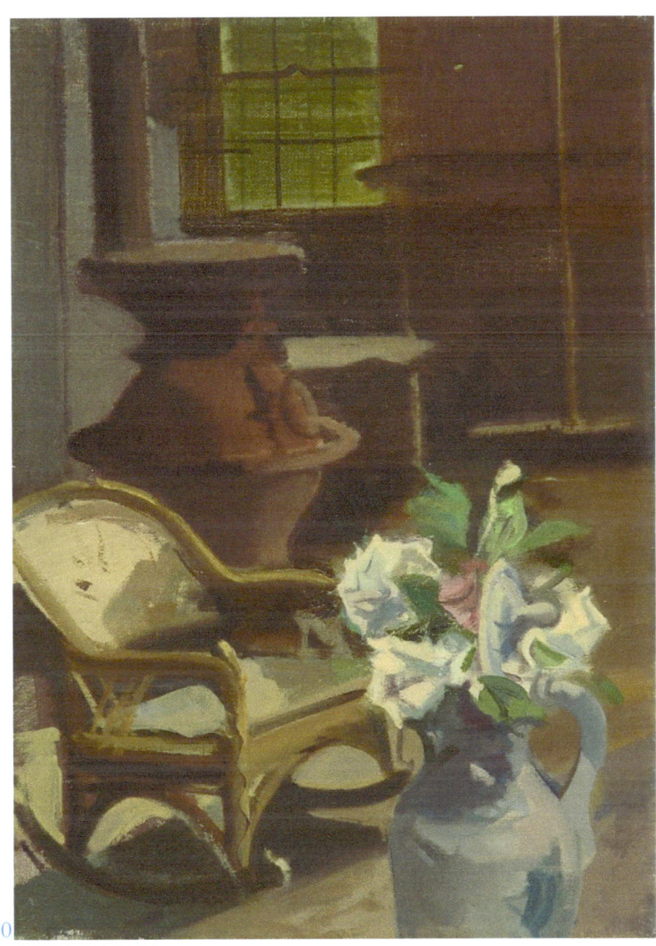

50

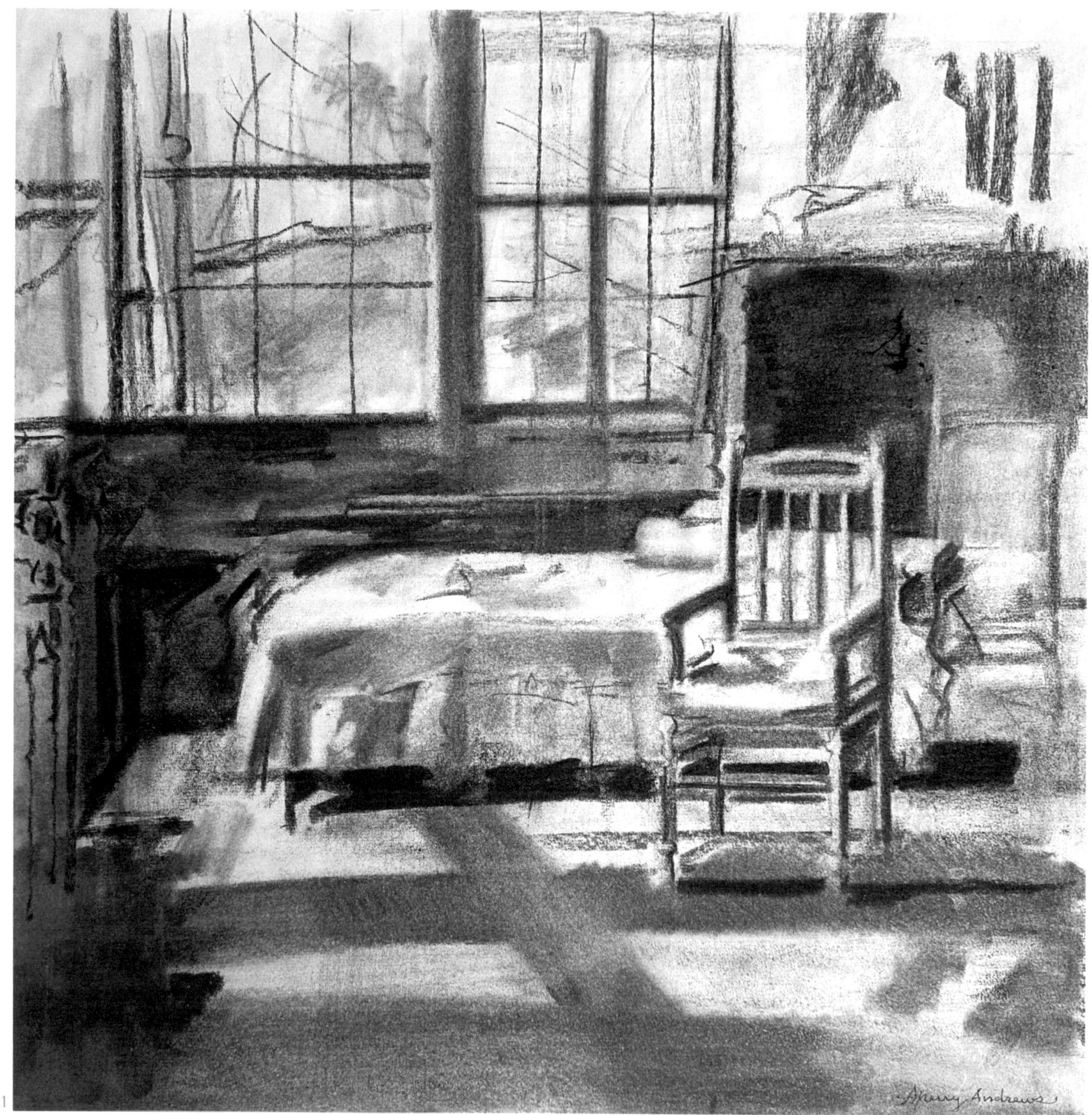

51

Sherry Andrews

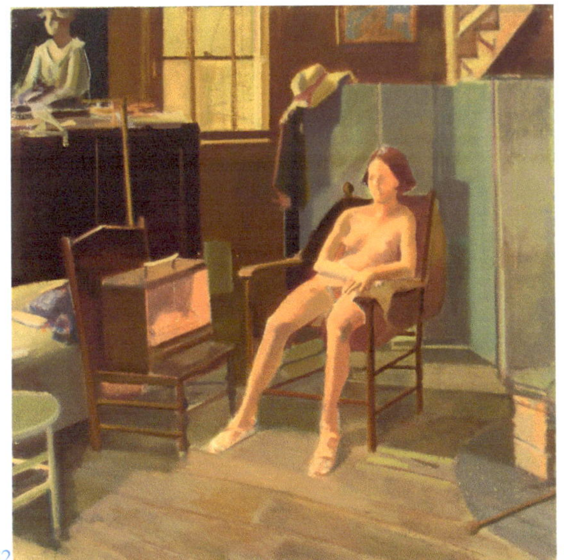

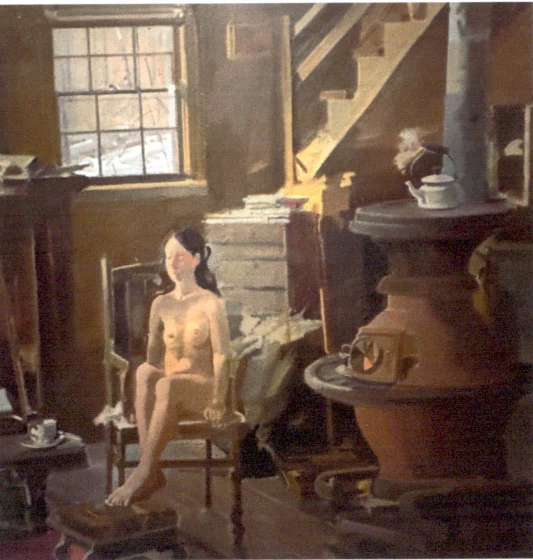

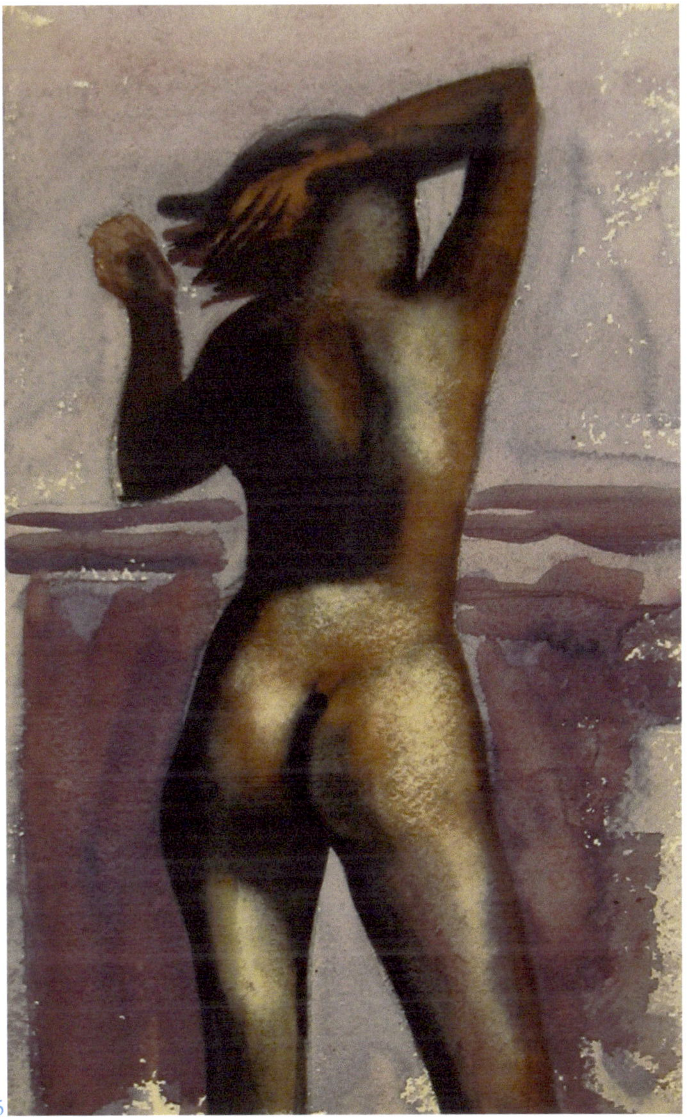

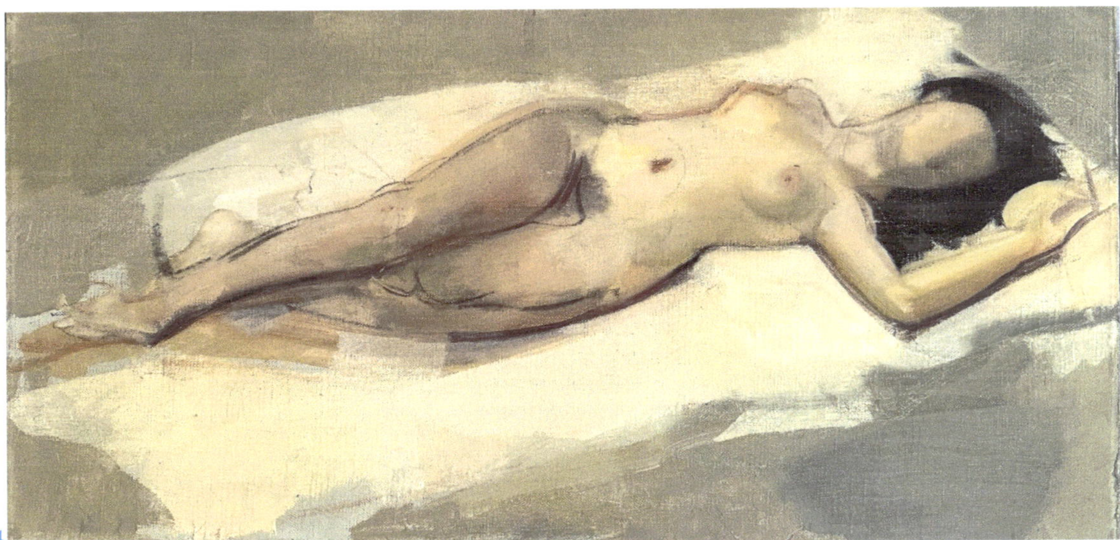

Four or five artists would get together in Sperry's studio to draw a model. I think we simply called up and figured out what was going on on a particular day. No set time, nothing formal, artists simply wandered in and out all day. In the winter the model sat close to the stove. She was absolutely bright red on one side and icy blue on the other. We kept rotating her in a vain attempt to keep her warm. We finally resorted to quick sketches so that she could move. I remember we were all bundled up in layers of sweaters and jackets but we were so intent on our drawings that we didn't let the cold bother us (C. Gibbons, private communication, August 29, 2005).

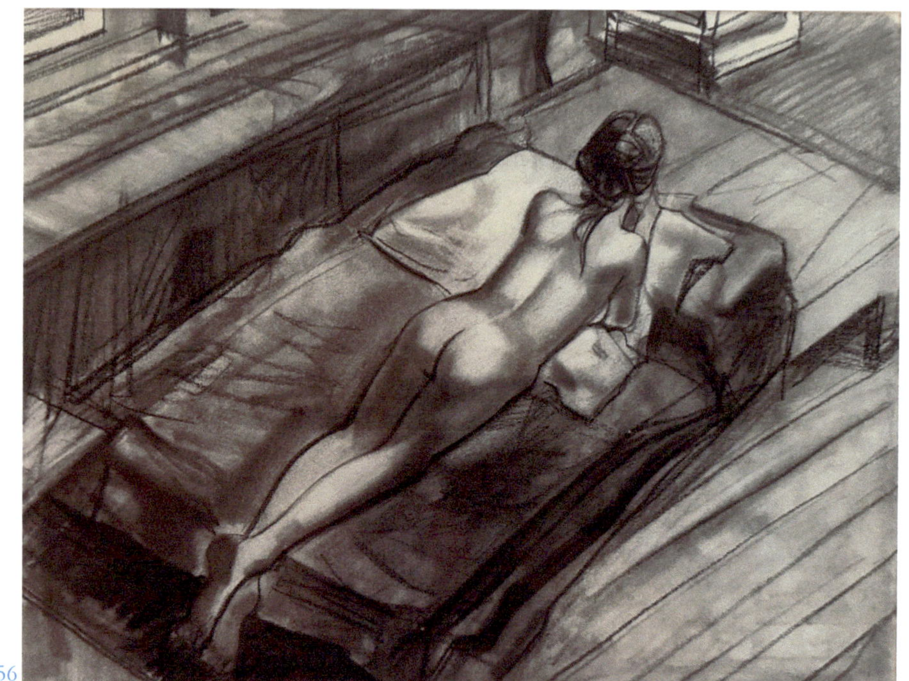

56

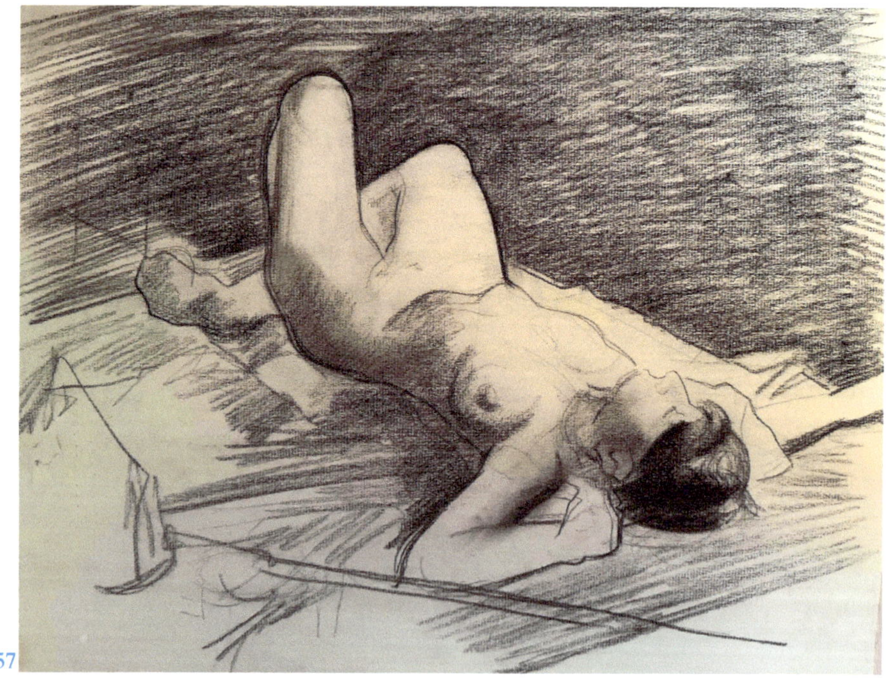

57

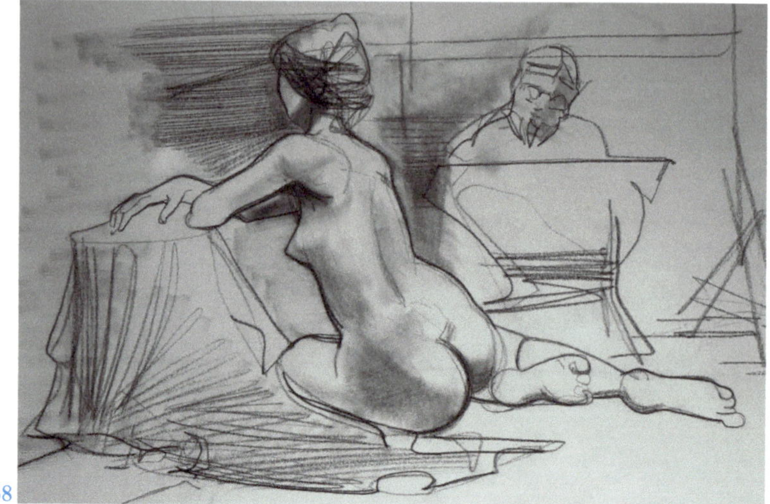

58

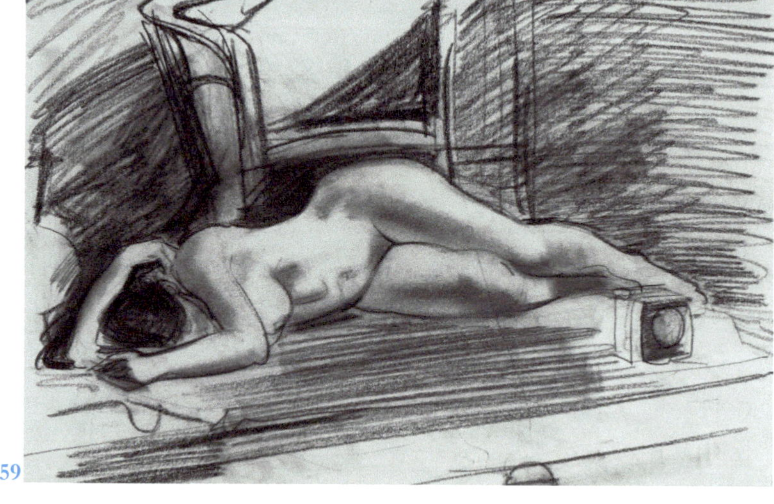

59

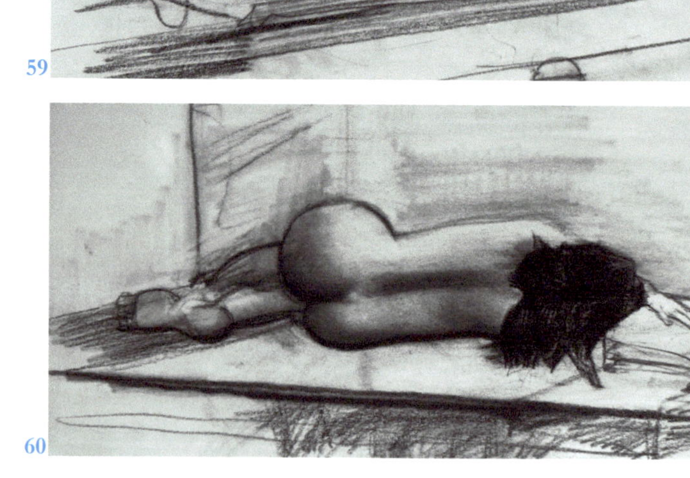

60

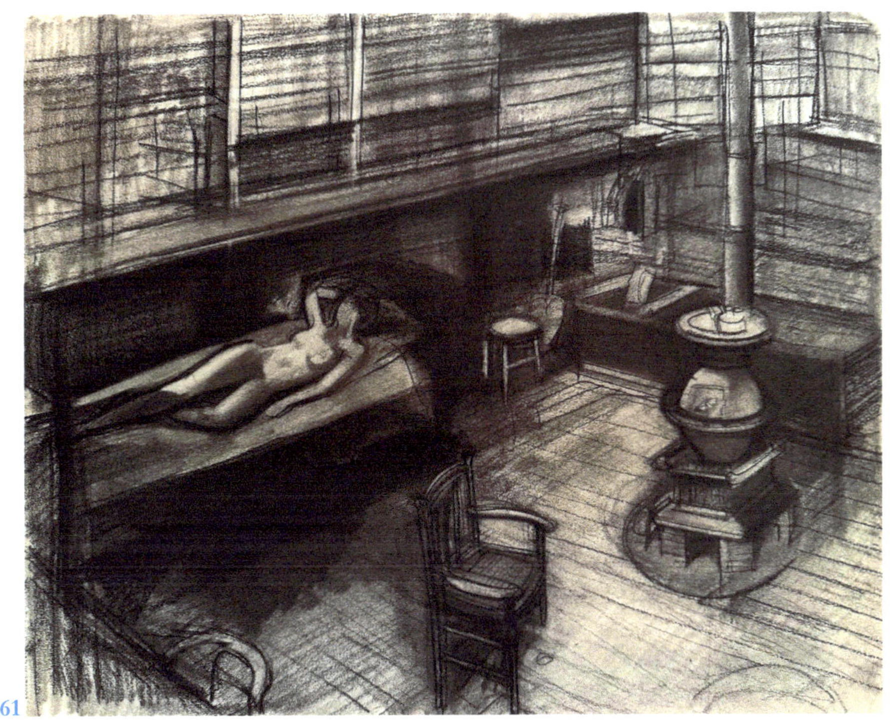

61

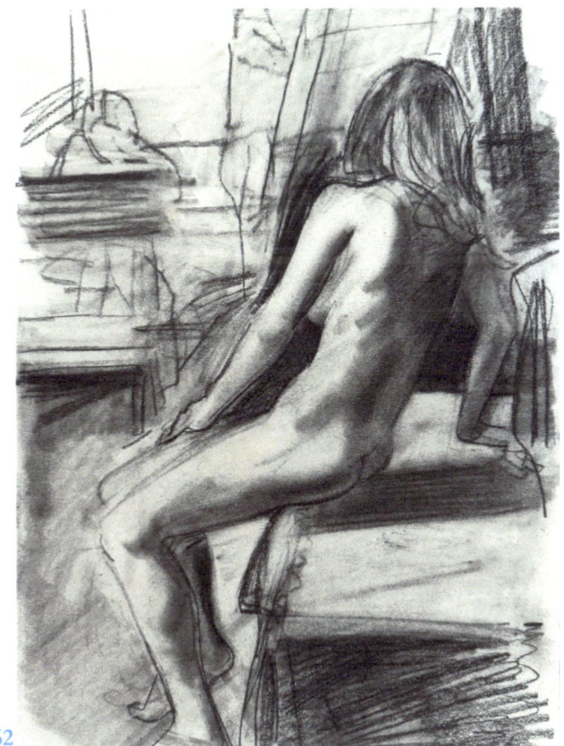

62

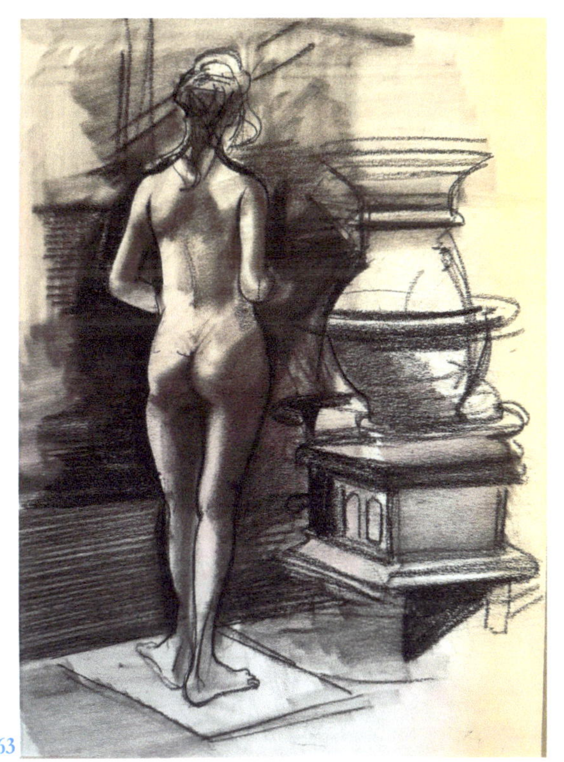

63

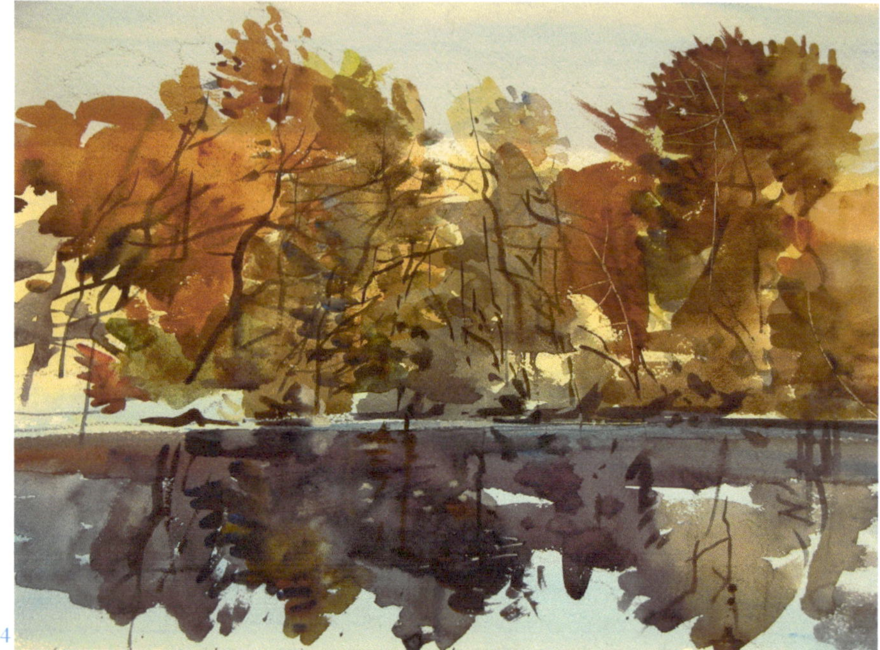

64

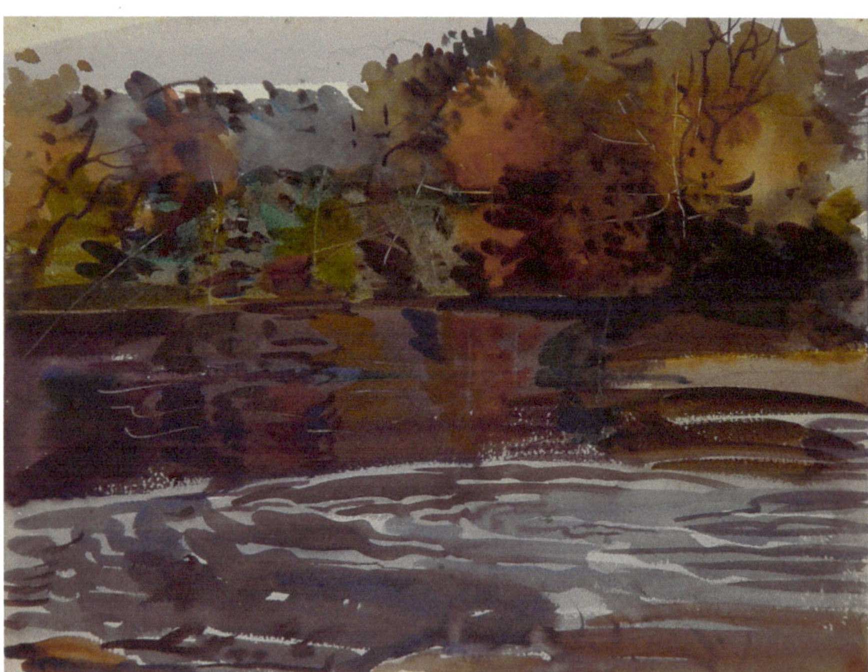

65

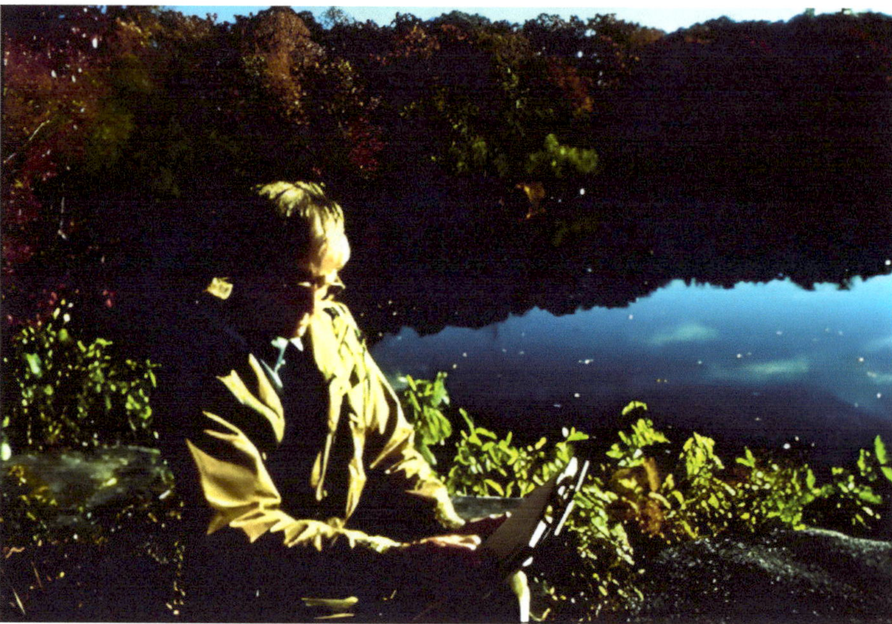

The right kind of paper is the paper that is right for your needs. A paper that behaves just the way you like it to act, this is very important to your direct action at a given moment. One cannot stress this point too lightly, often the difference between a successful attack, or a rout. Remember the brush need not rub the paper at all, so to say. You mix the wash that you think will match the tones in the object, or objects you are looking at (notes, April 6, 1977).

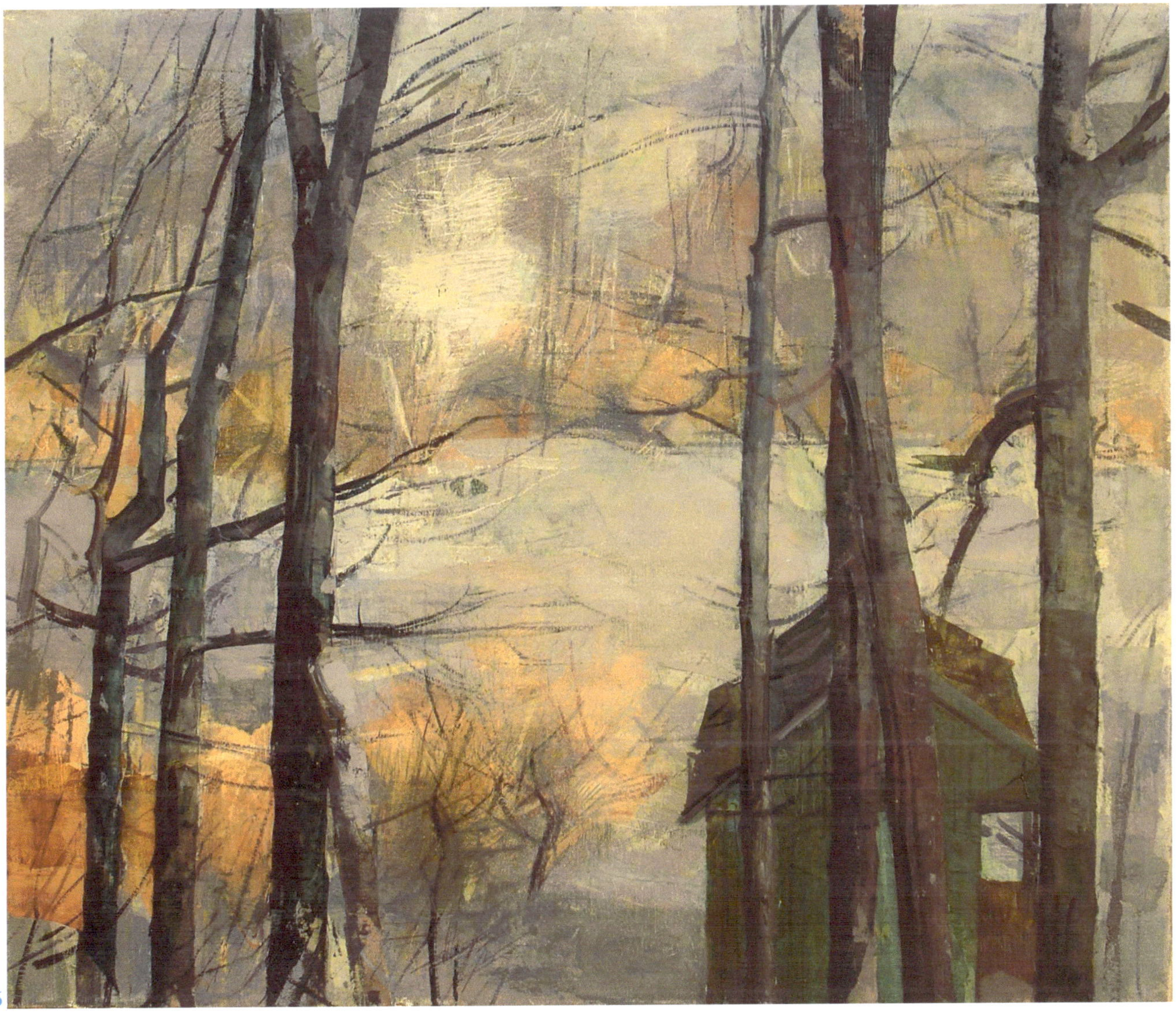

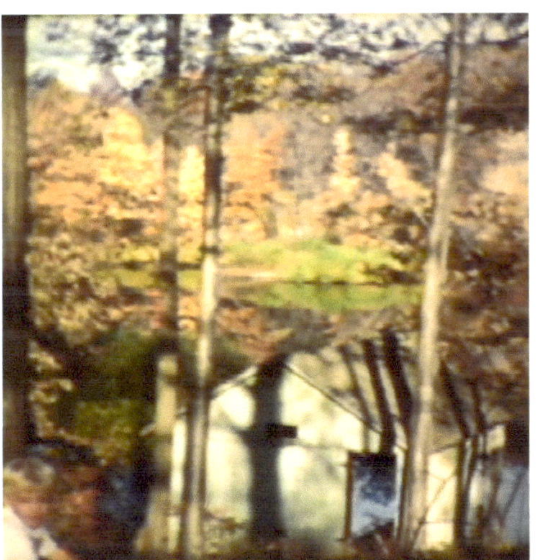

66

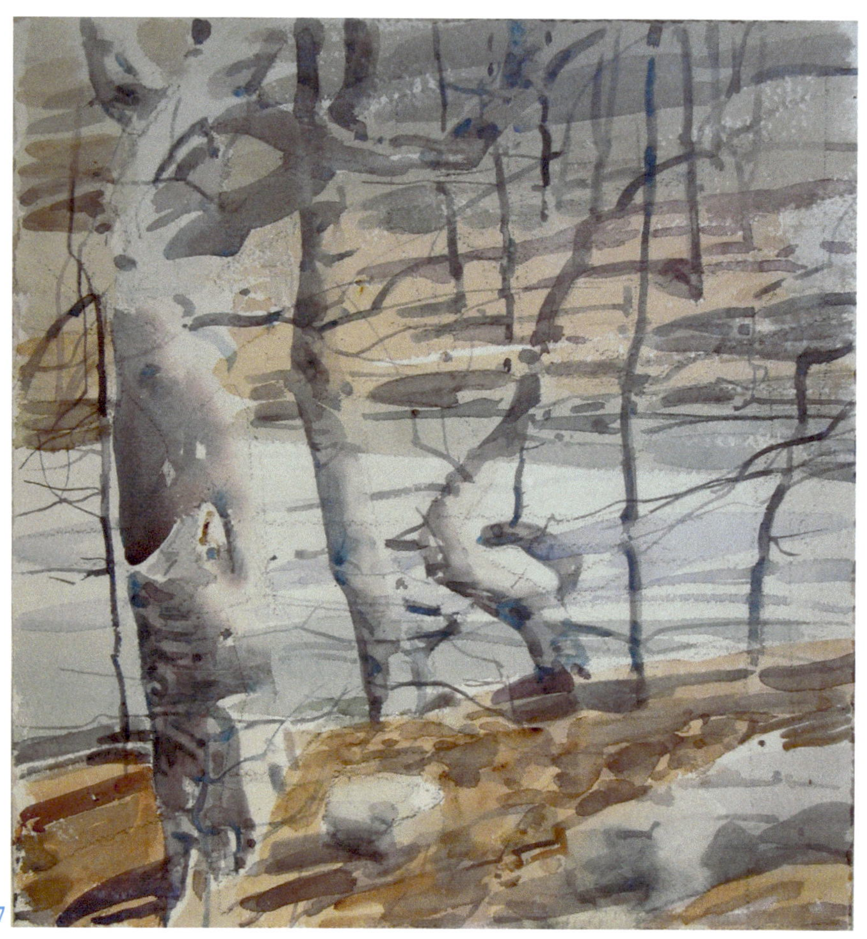

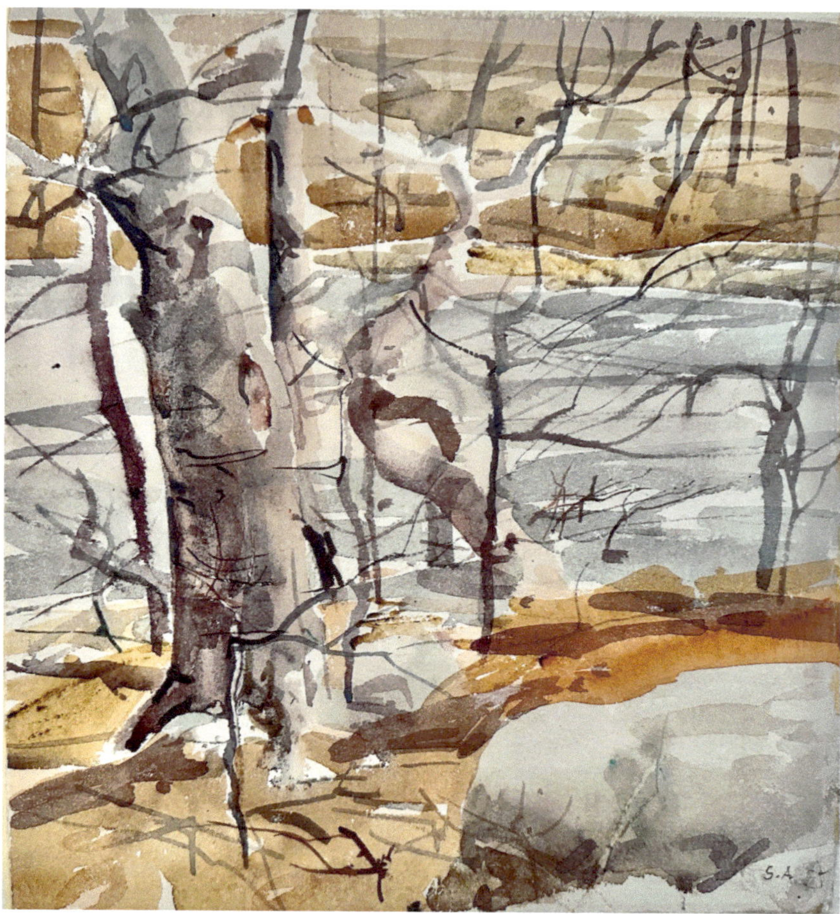

Monet's idea of returning again and again to the same location on successive days was such a pursuit. Not only did this give him the inner calm which added strength to his pursuits, but at the same time gave him more chances to arrange to reach his individual likes (notes, April 6, 1977).

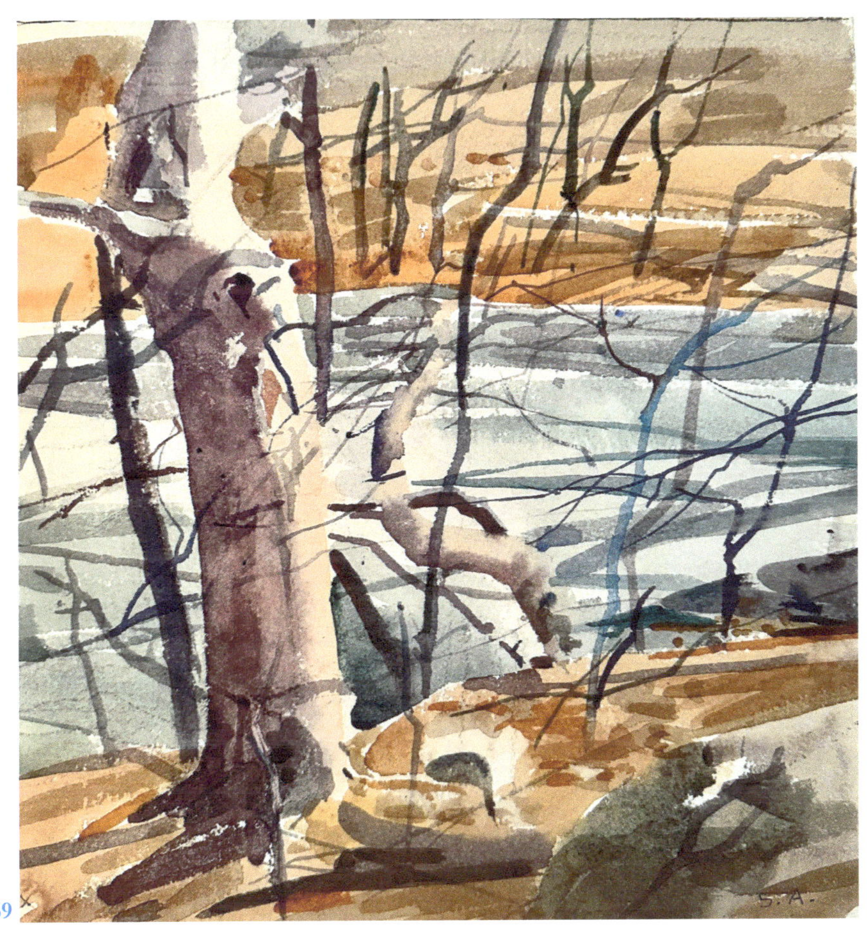

69

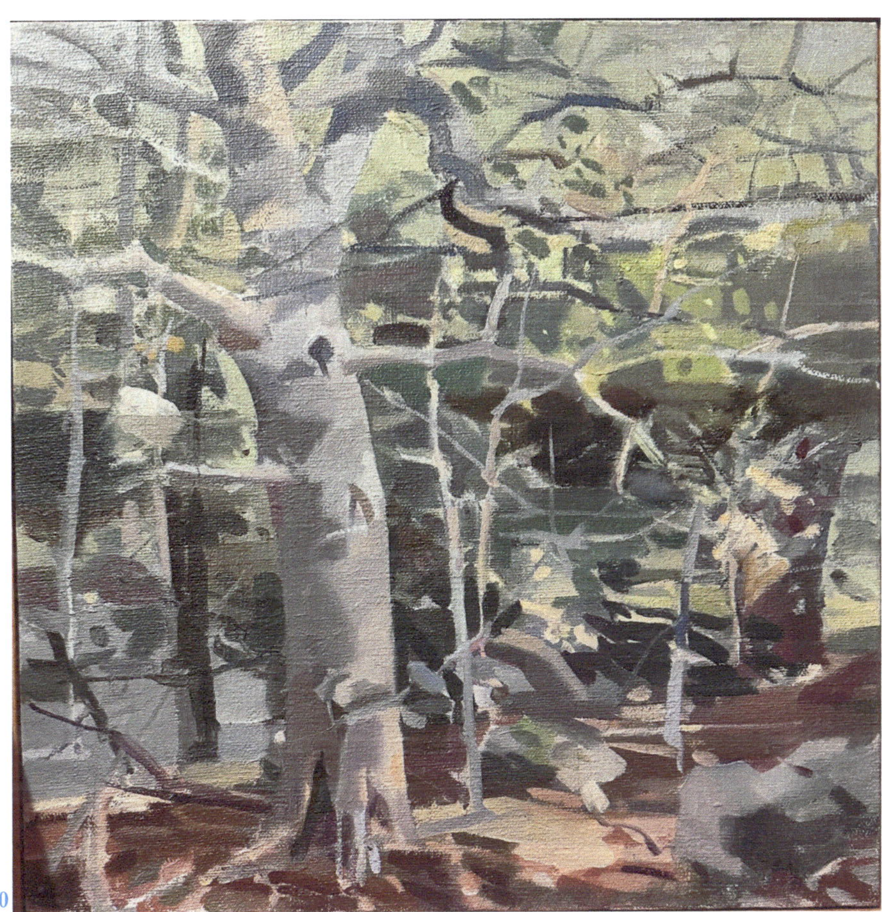

70

55

T.V. set. turning around I continued along the east of the pond, keeping the pond in sight on my left. I examined briefly the camp sight on the knoll to the east of the pond. CAMP SIGHT / POND

Then the path to the dam. Here there have been some changes since our visit there last summer. The tree which you were concerned about is still in the same position, not resting yet, on the edge of the second Dam. Upon the Dam itself another tree lies directly across the Dam

POND SURFACE — DAM PATH — OLD FALLEN TREE — FALLEN TREE — SECOND DAM —

and extends out over the water of the pond. the tree has been up-rooted from the base of the trunk, perhaps by the violent wind storm we had here late last Fall. The Pond itself is very high now, the over flow near the large white rock

71

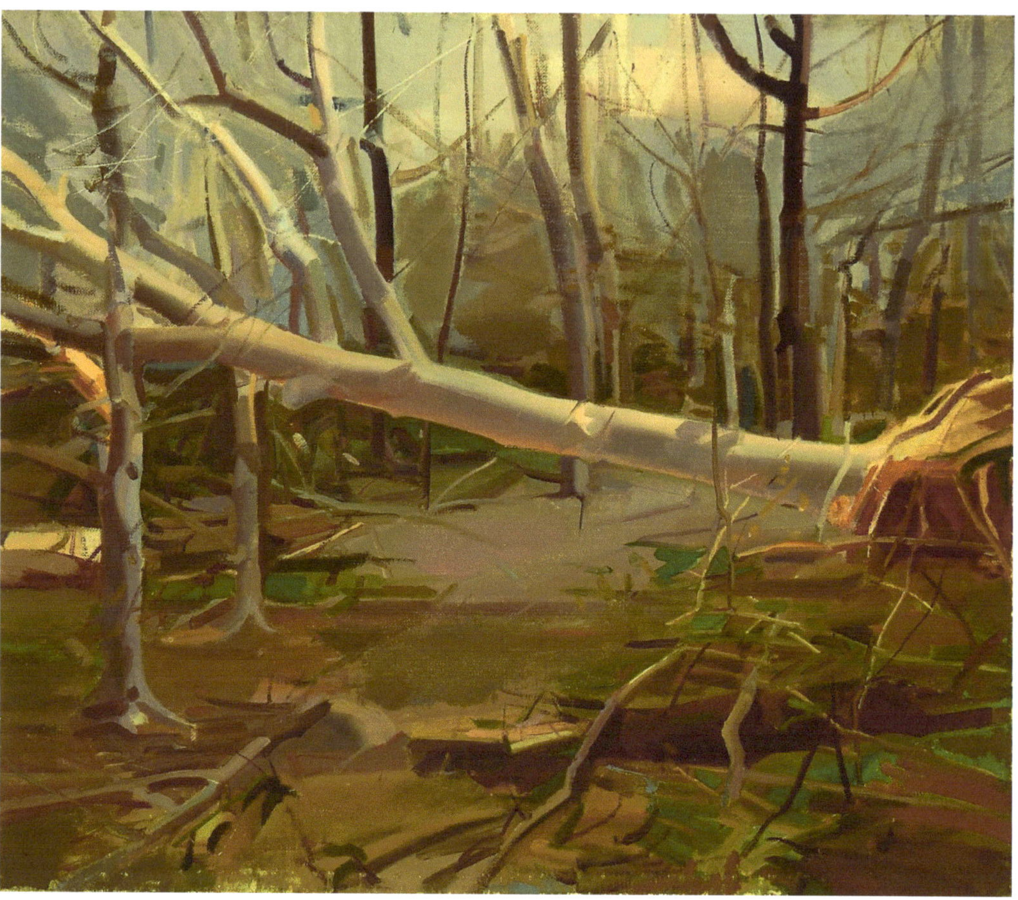

Here there have been some changes since our visit there last summer. The tree which you were concerned about is still in the same position, now resting gently on the edge of the second dam. Upon the dam itself another tree lies directly across the dam and extends out over the water of the pond. The tree has been uprooted from the base of the trunk, perhaps from the violent wind storm we had here late last fall. The pond itself is very high now, the over flow near the large white rock is running well, the only sound at that moment one could hear. . . . I approached the road turning towards the house, stopped for a few minutes at the cemetery to admire the home, so proud and handsome against the late light in the West. (Letter to the author, February 2, 1975)

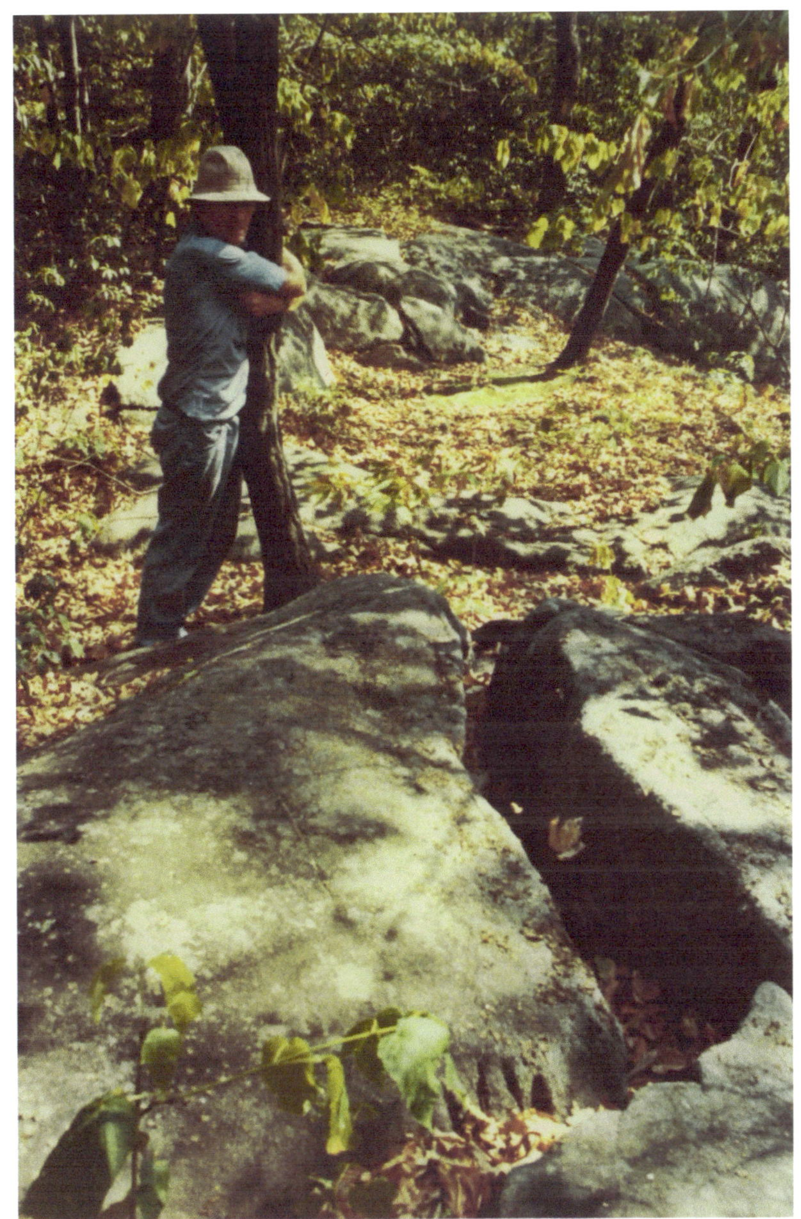

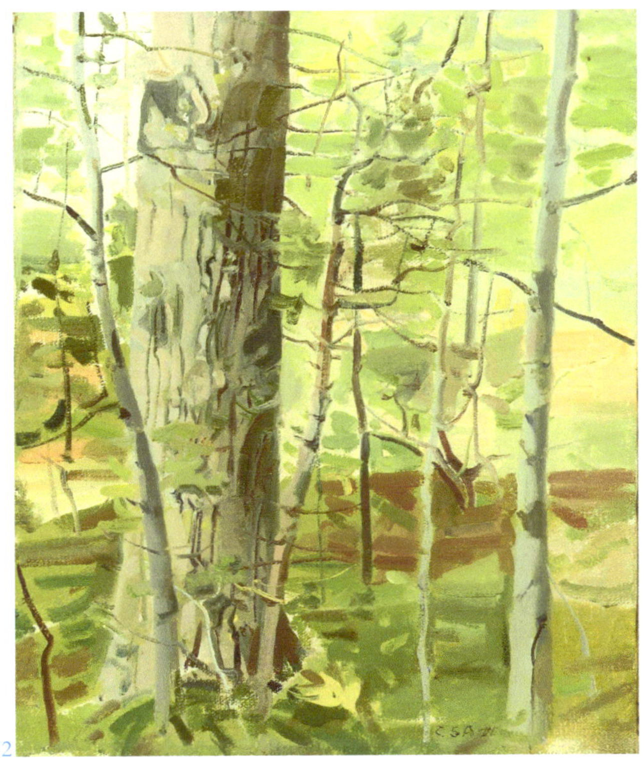

72

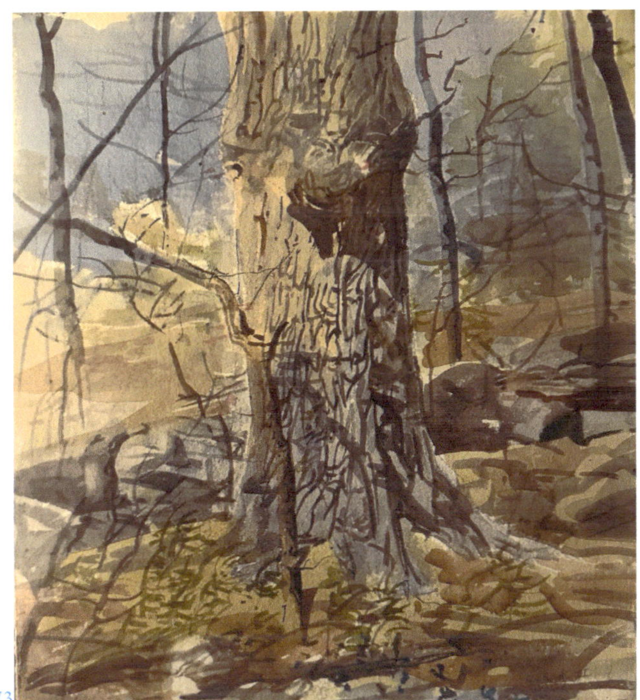

73

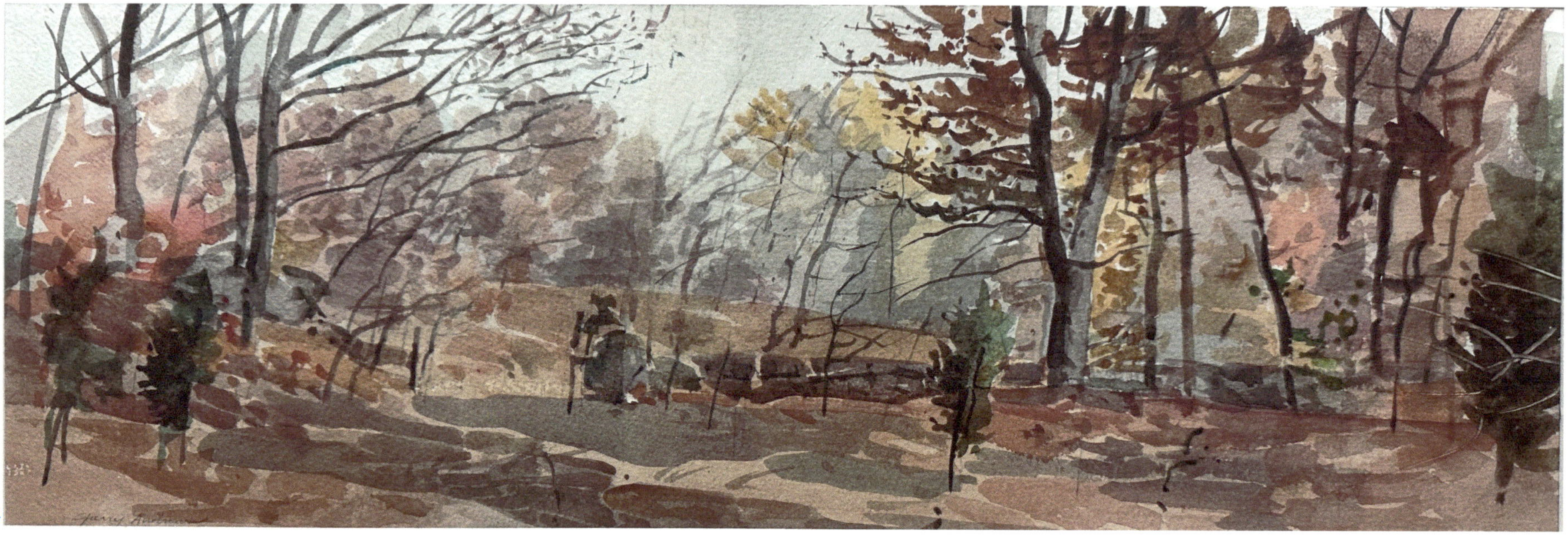

74

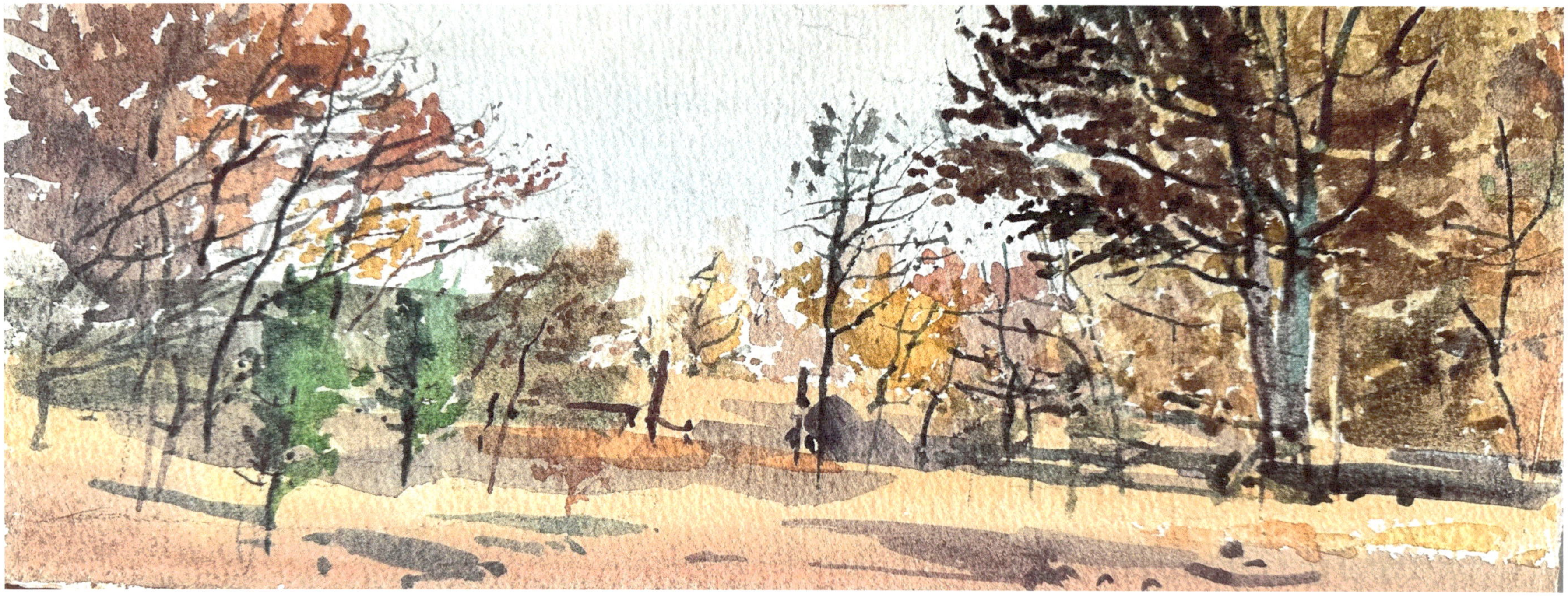

75

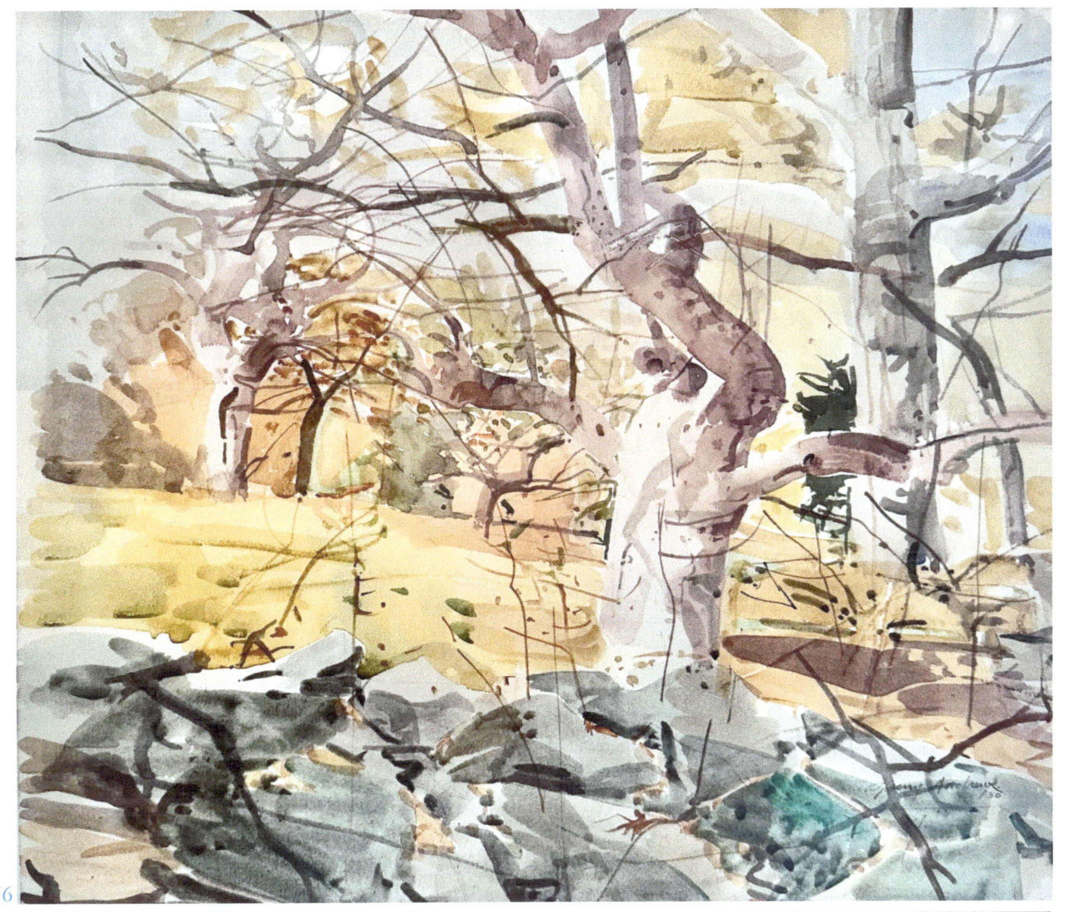

76

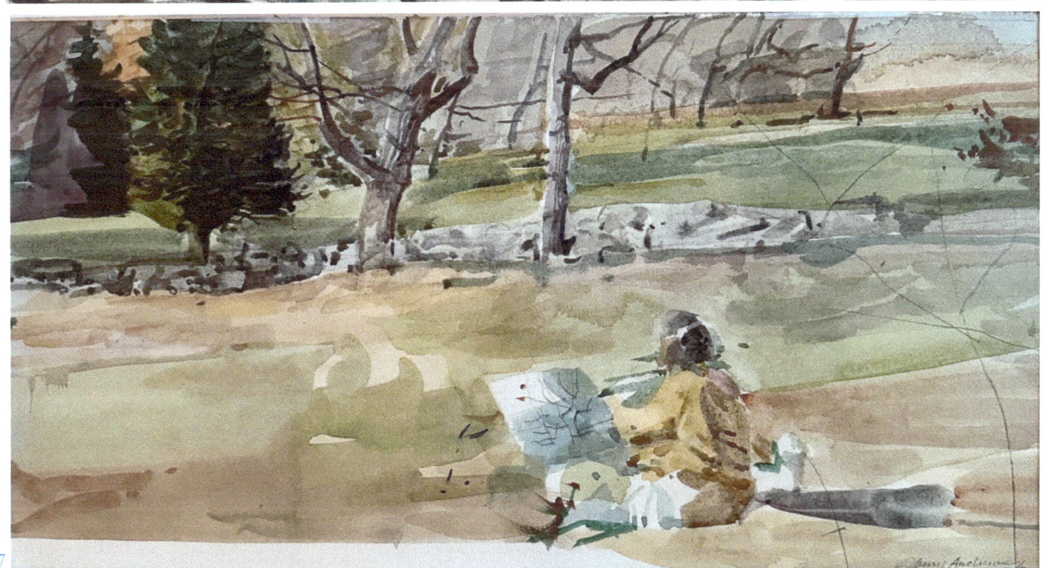

77

59

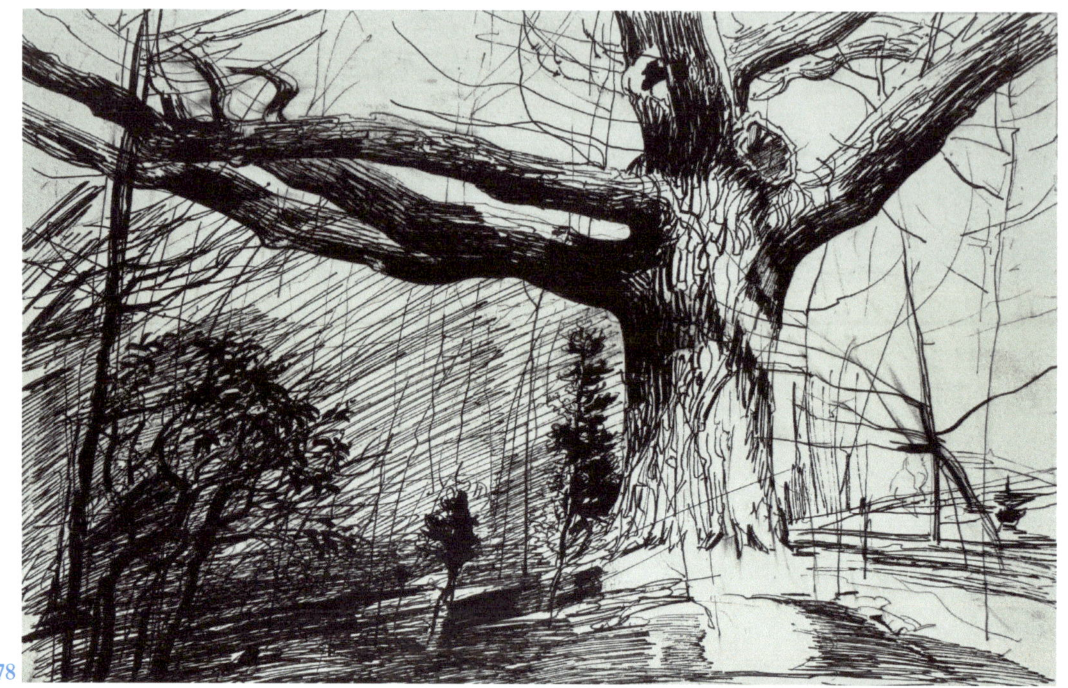

78

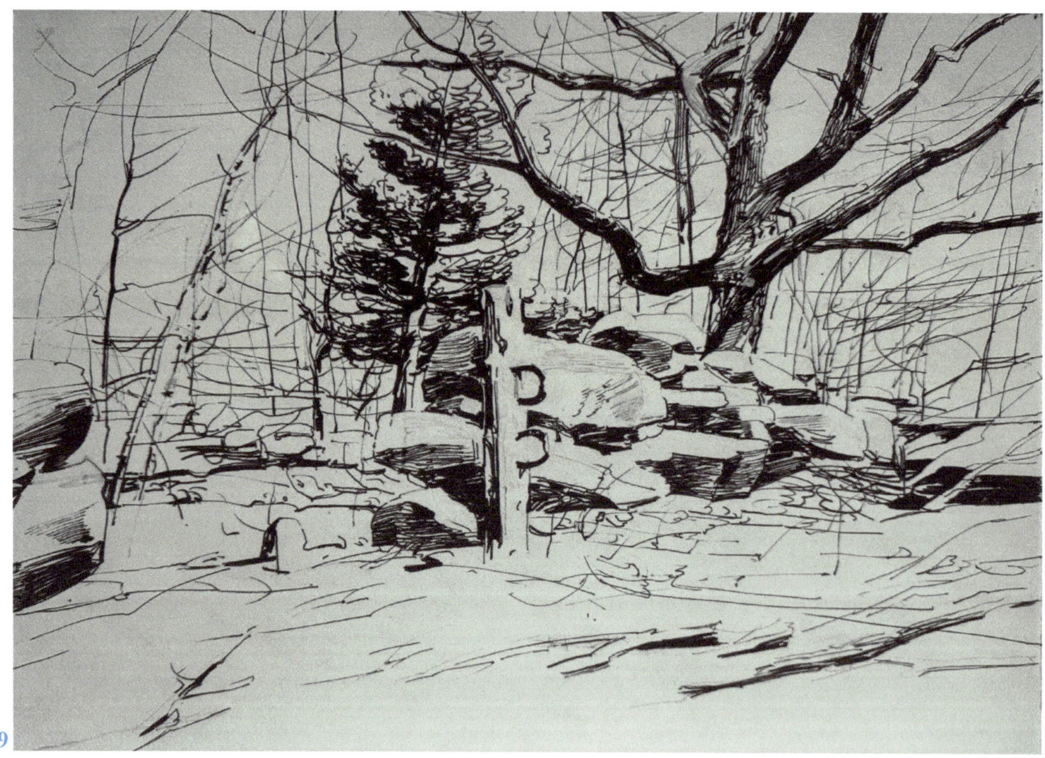

79

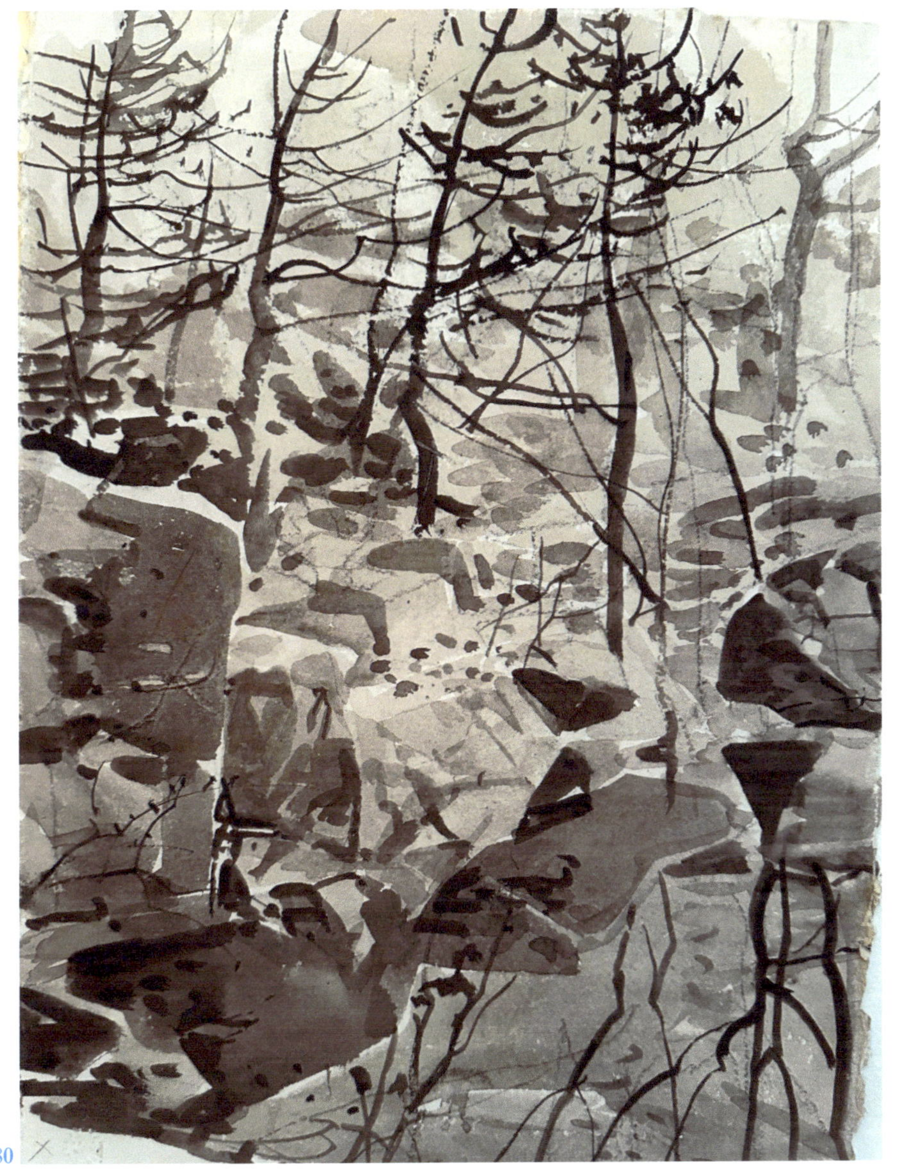

80

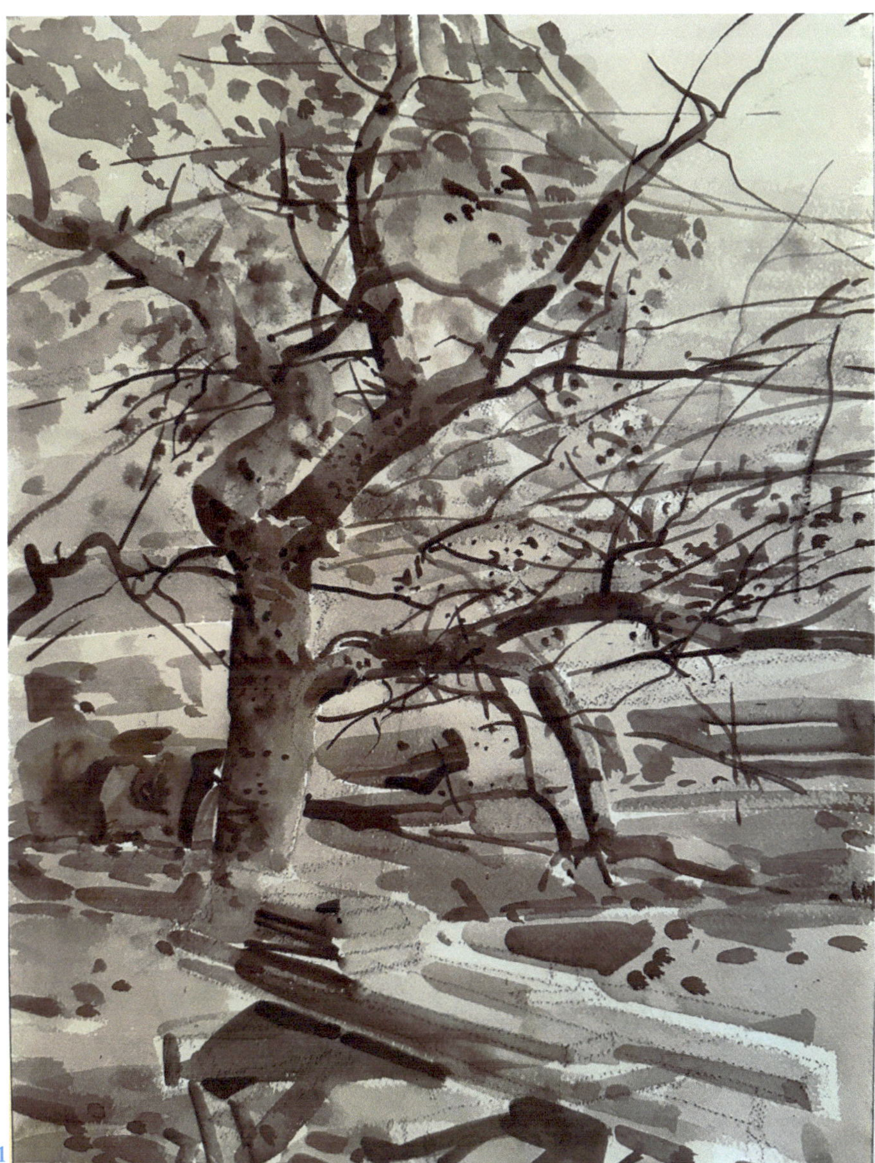

81

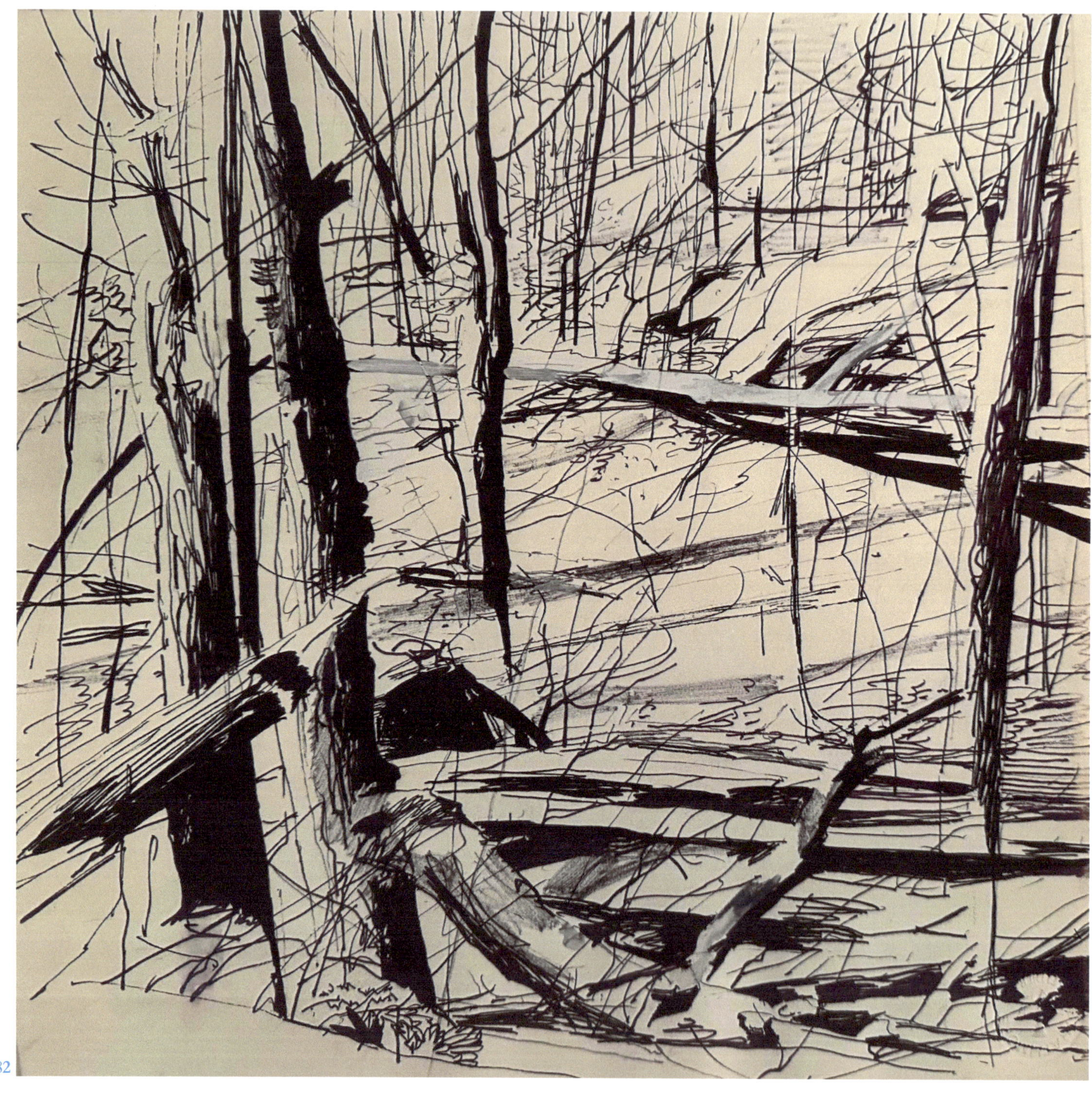

62

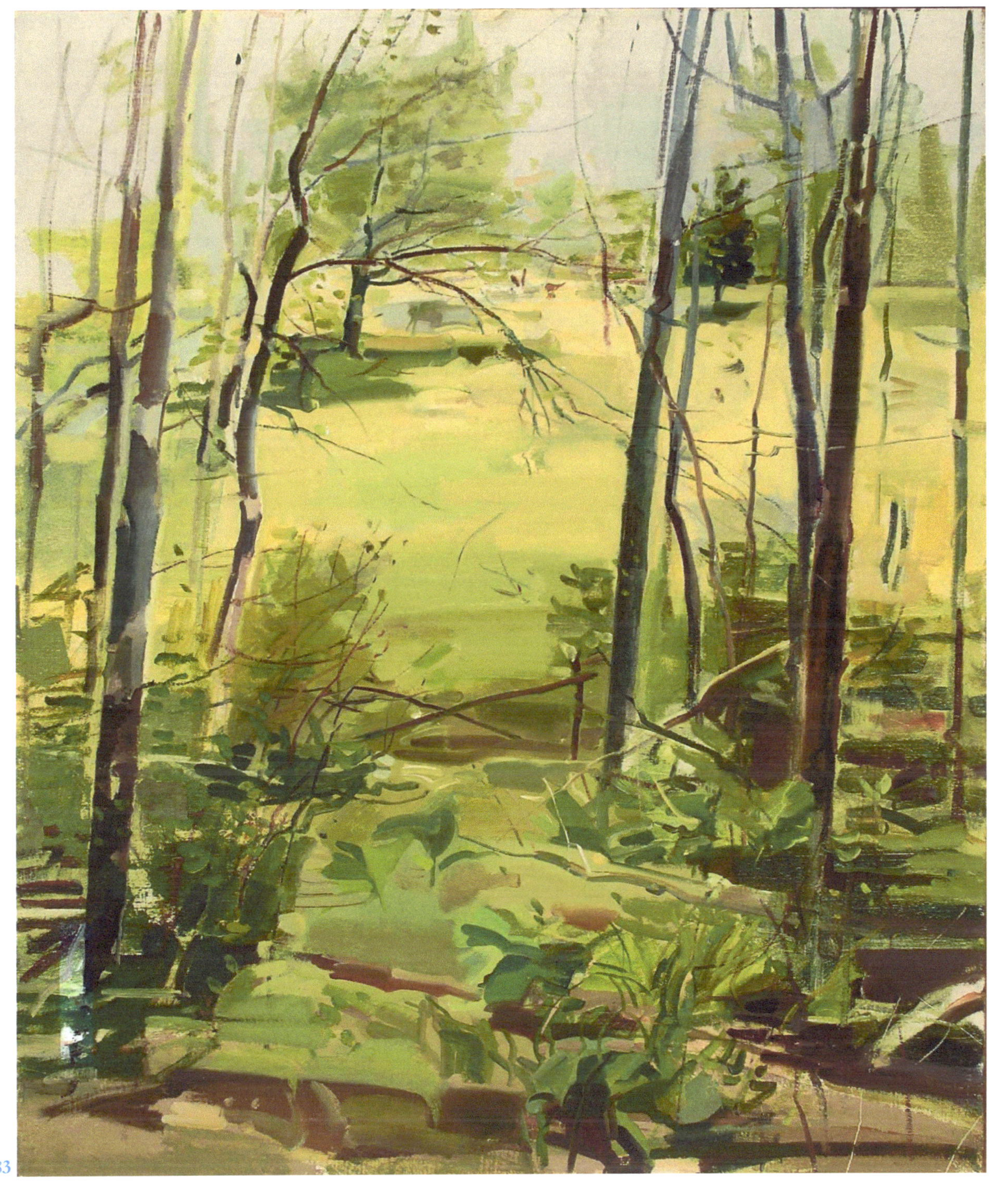

83

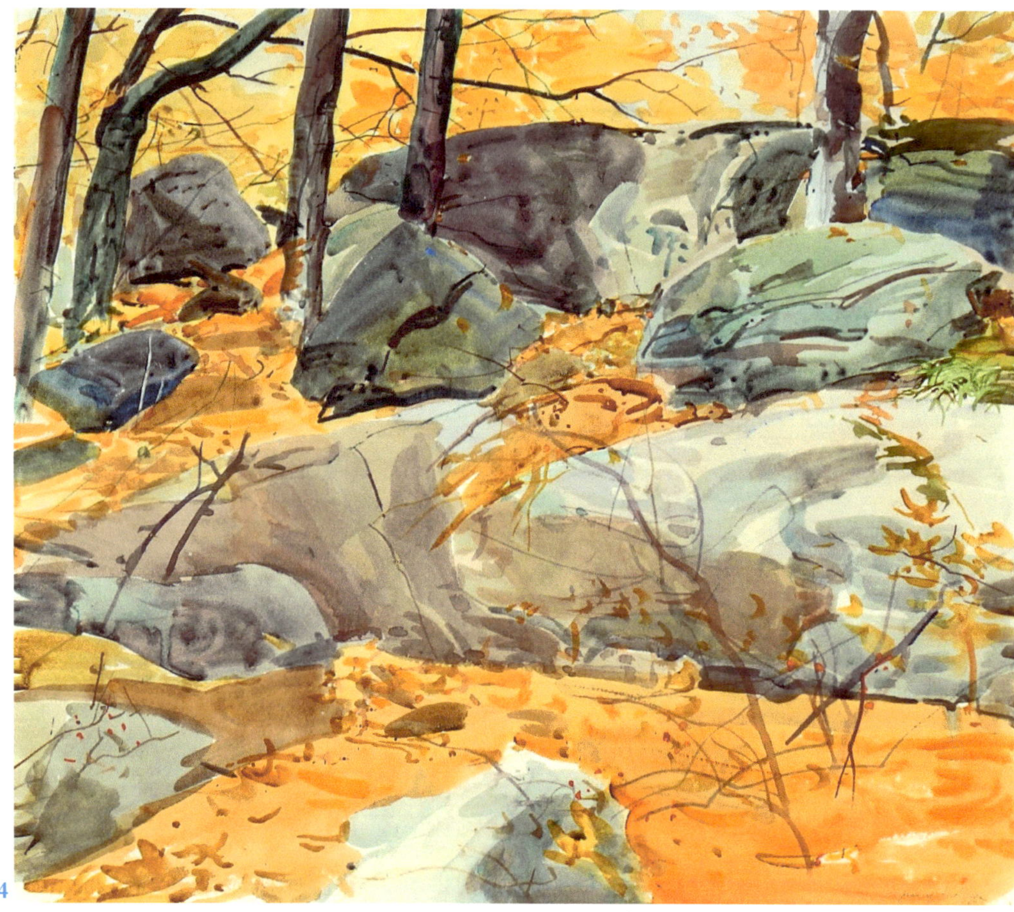

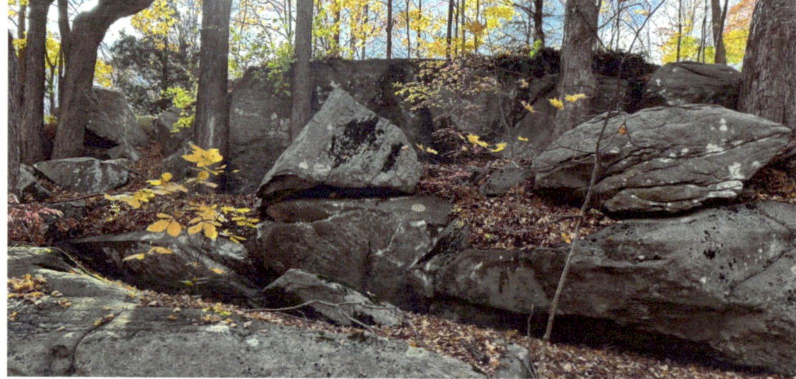

You want the first commitment to come close to your desires. This may not always happen of course, but it is very satisfying when it does. Make the observation, yet do not attempt too much. It is important to be ready to spot the moment (notes, April 6, 1977).

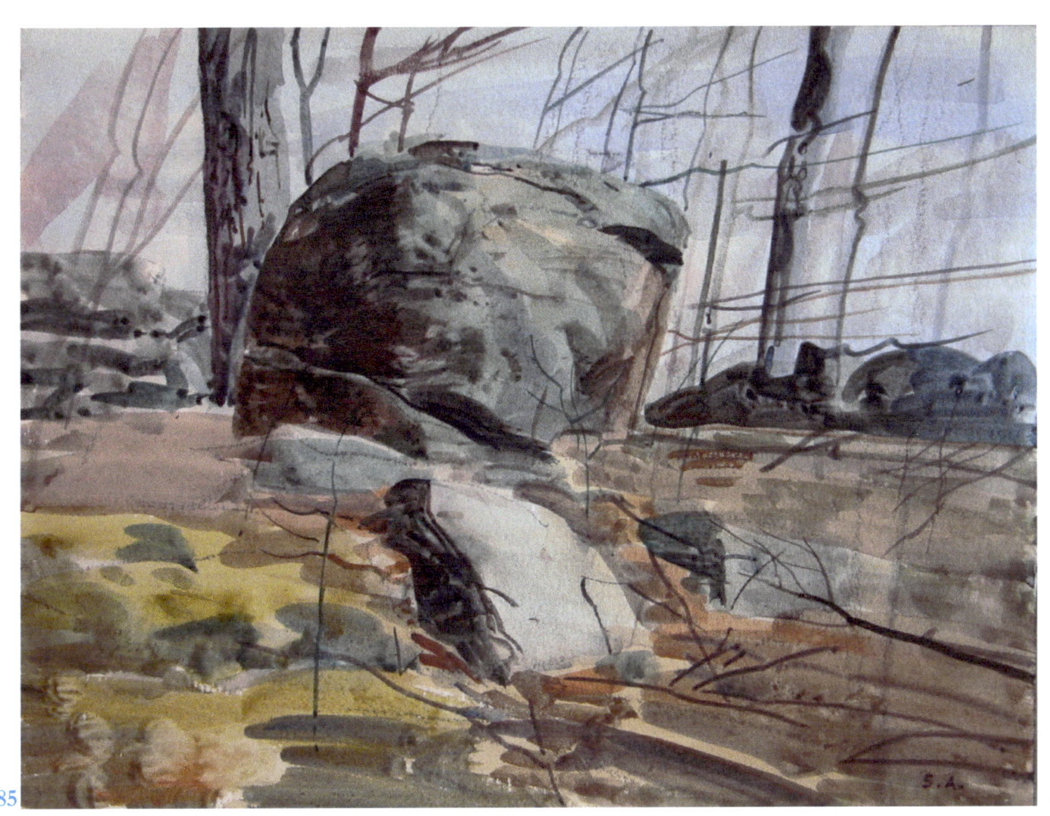

85

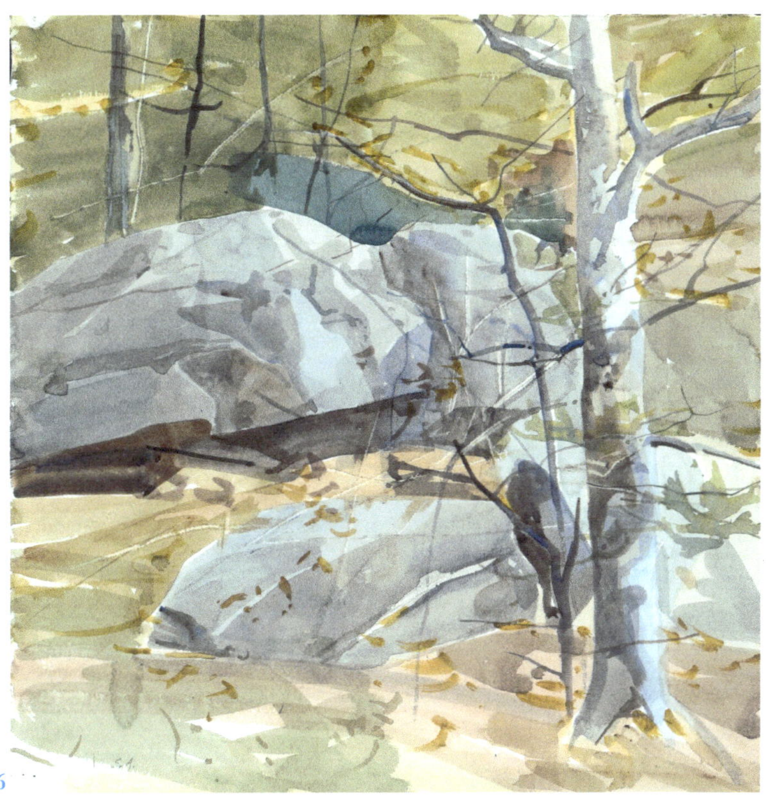

86

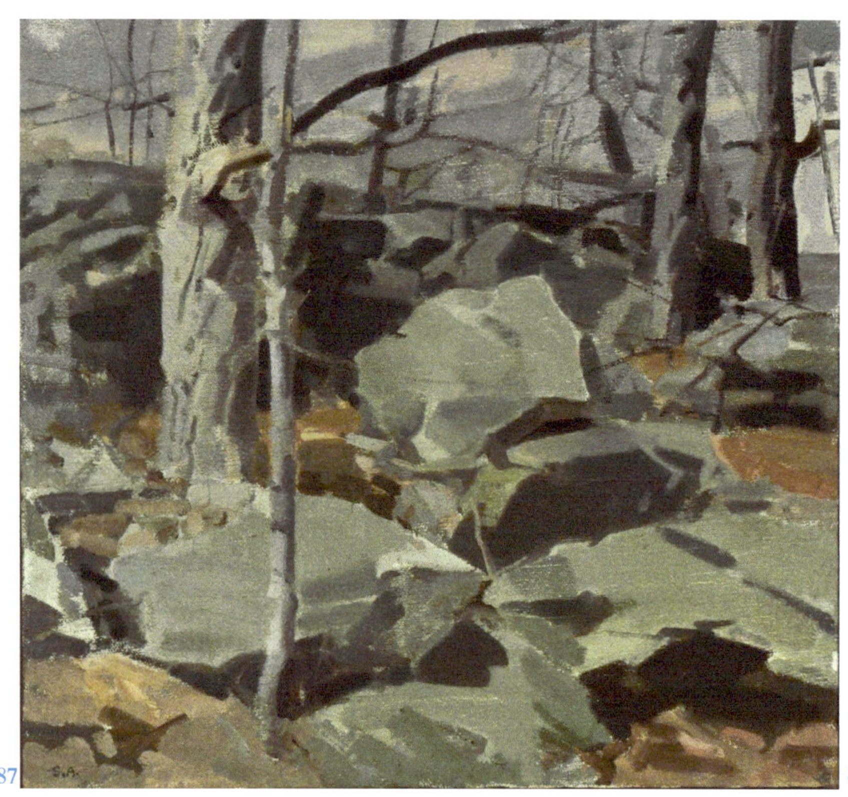

87

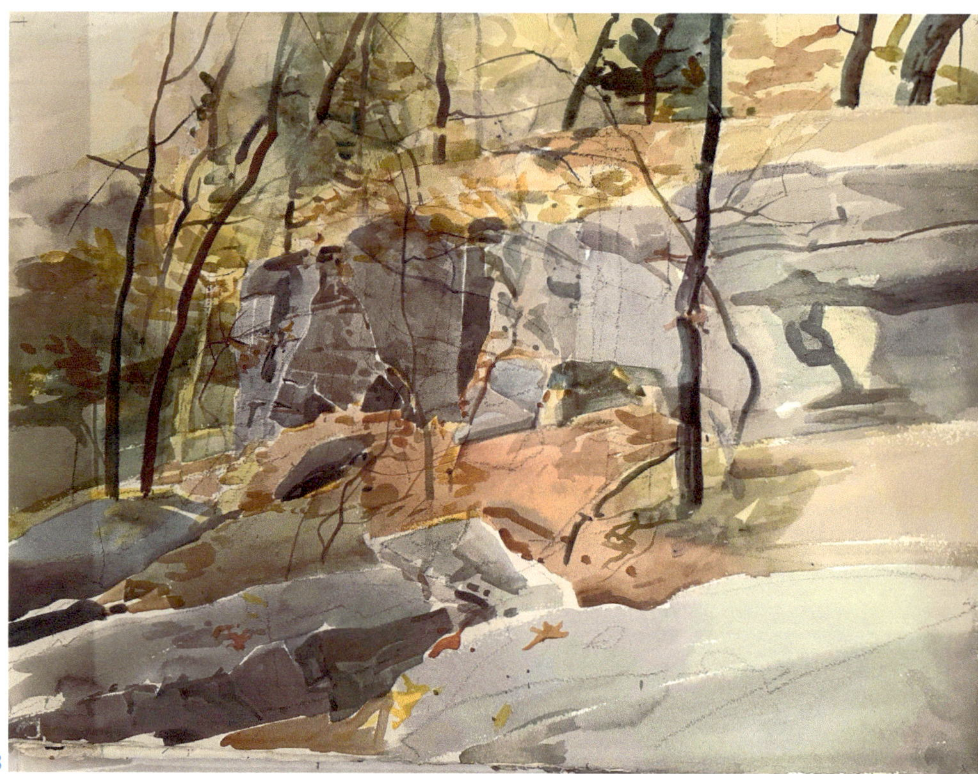

88

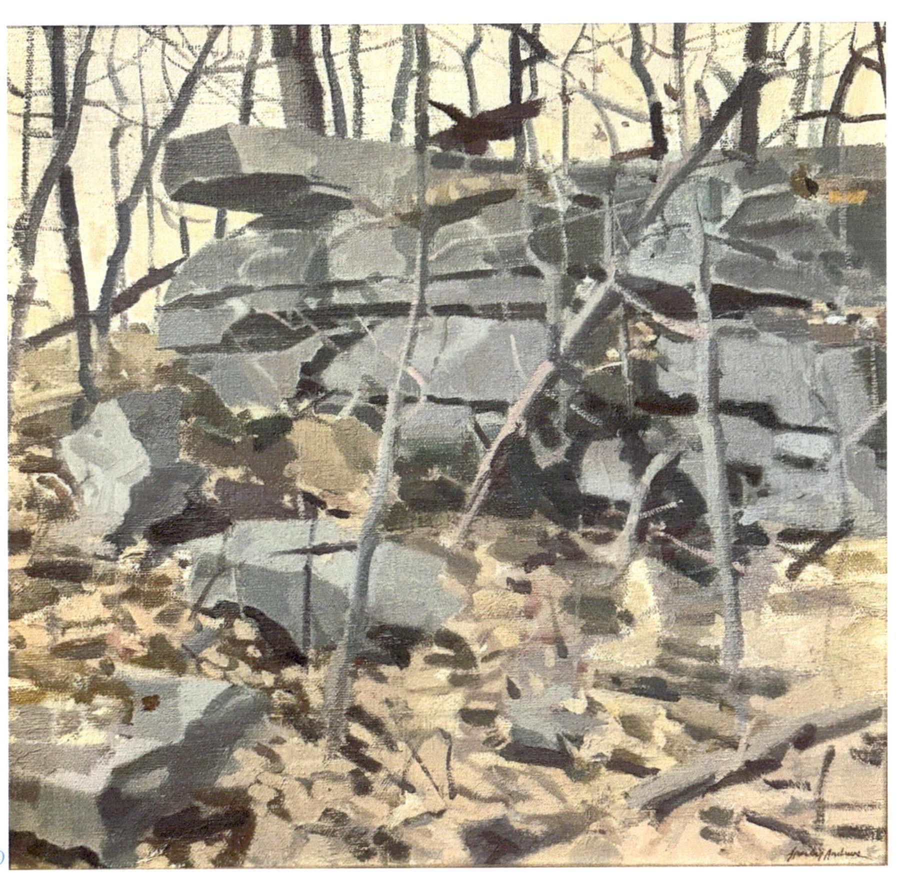

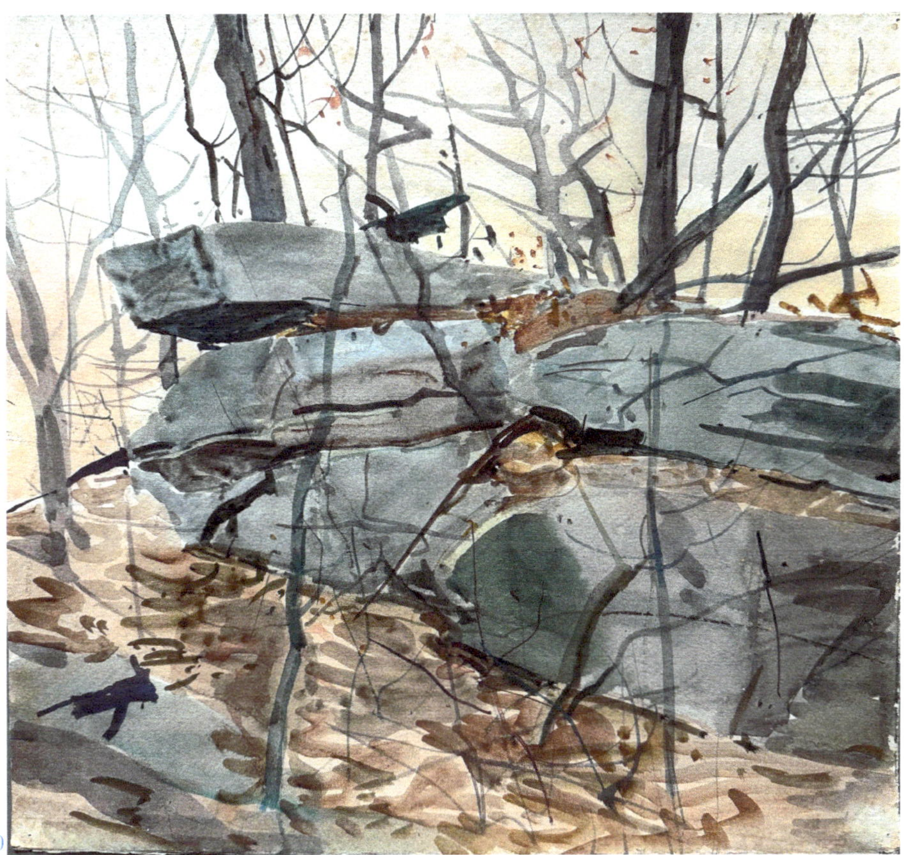

Try a study when the weather is low, a kind of dullness will often lead to a better reading of different planes of color, lights and darks are more apparent. Lights and values do not change so rapidly. Weather can be an important advantage (notes, May 9, 1977).

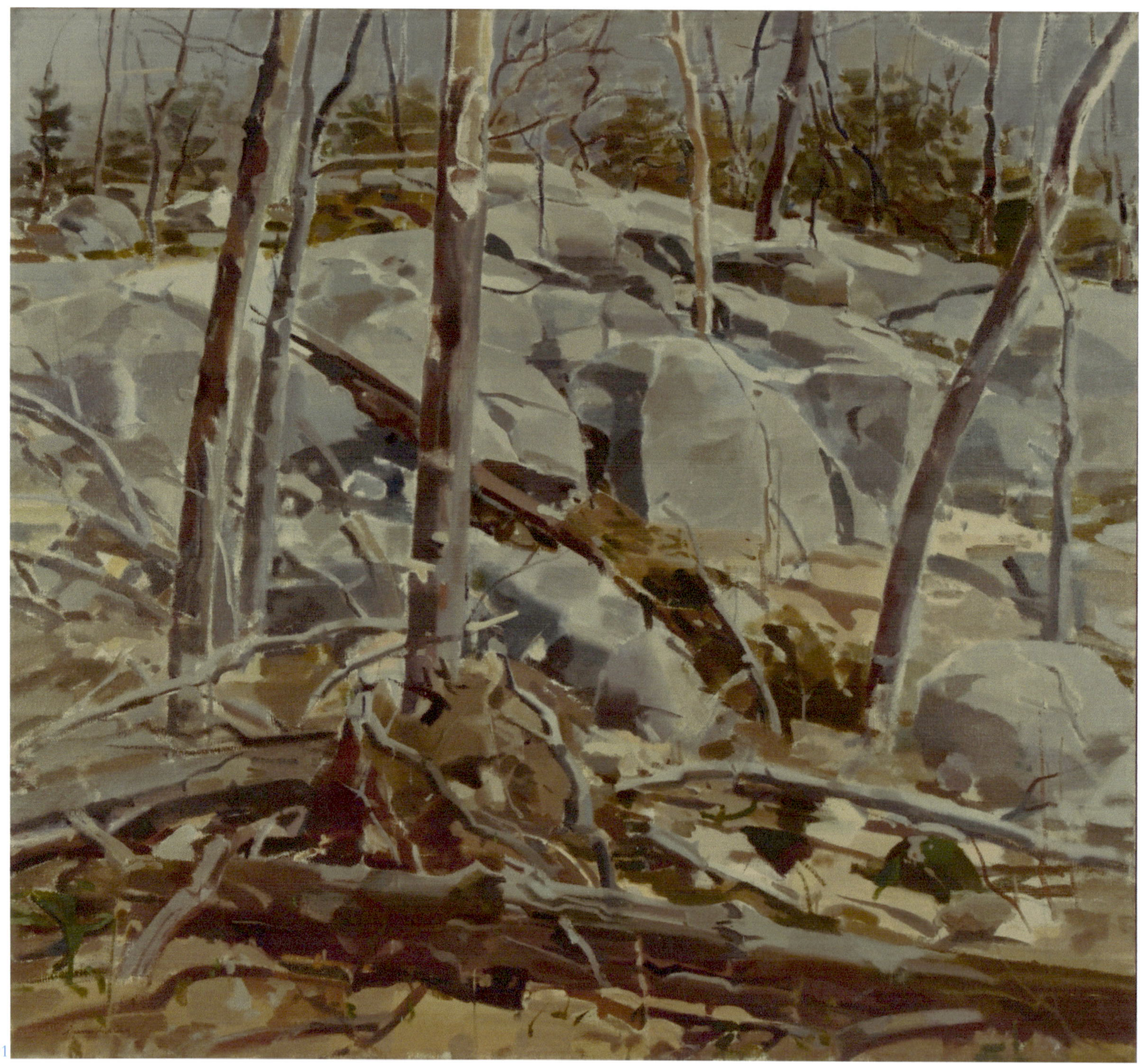

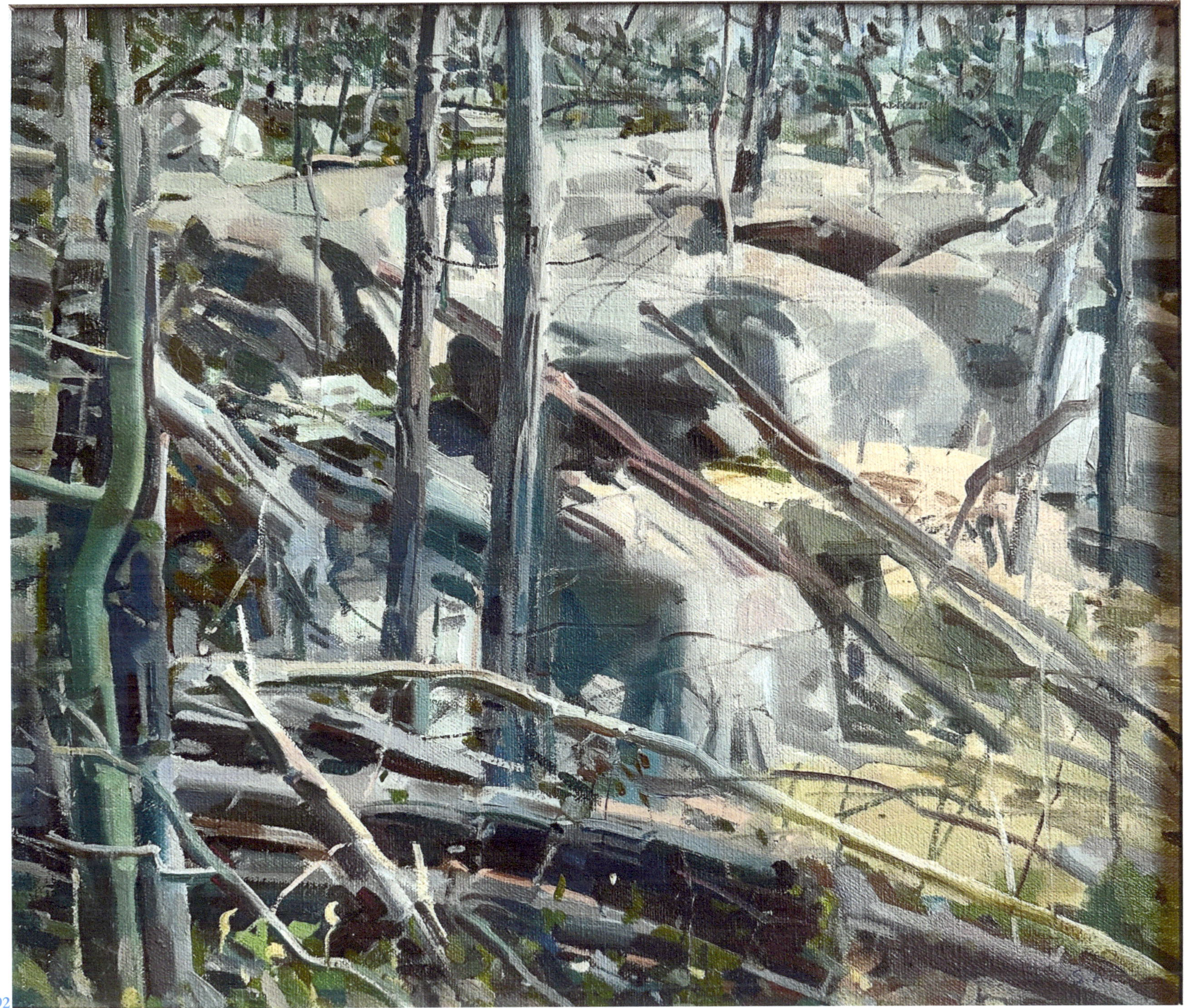

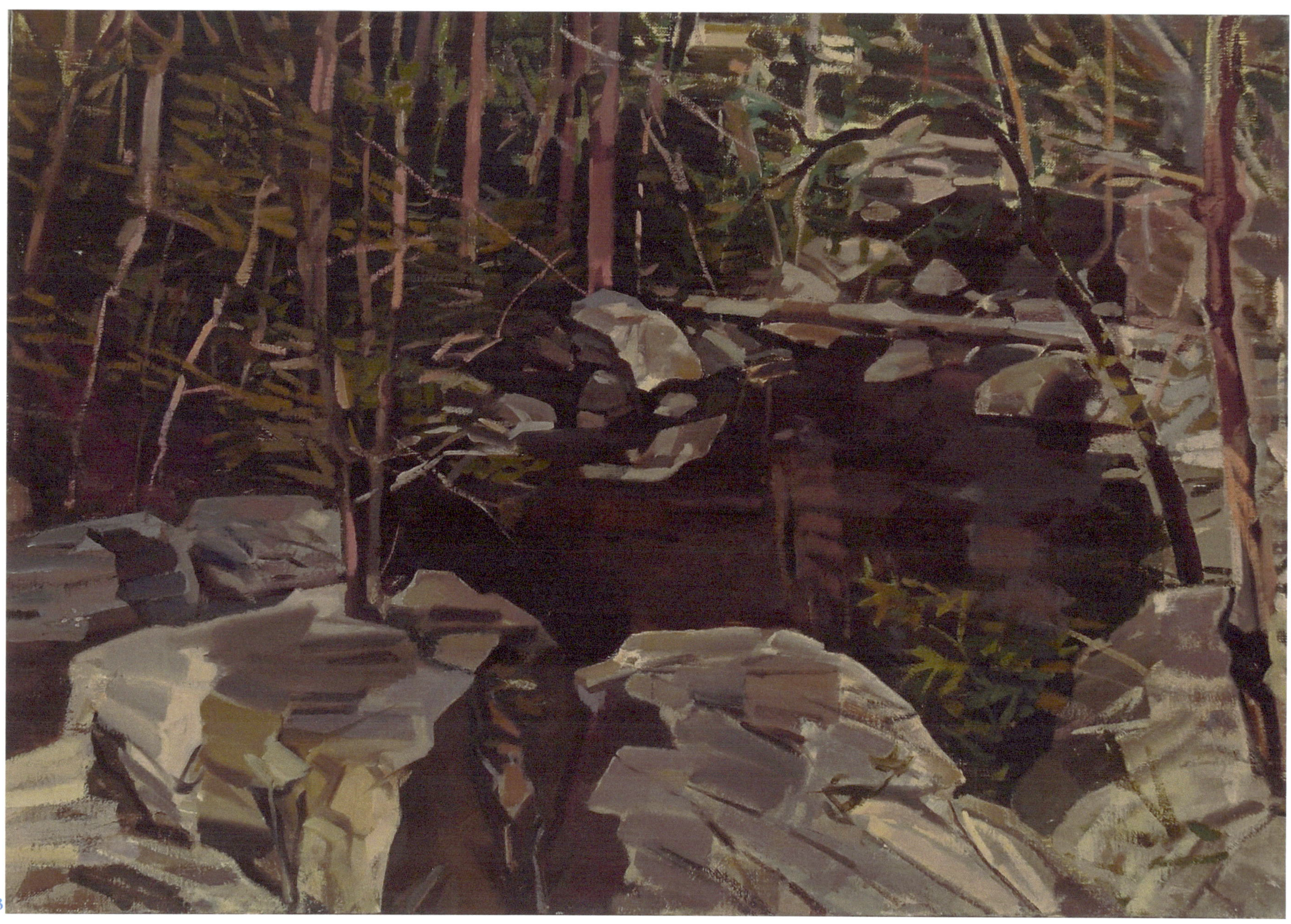

Cora's

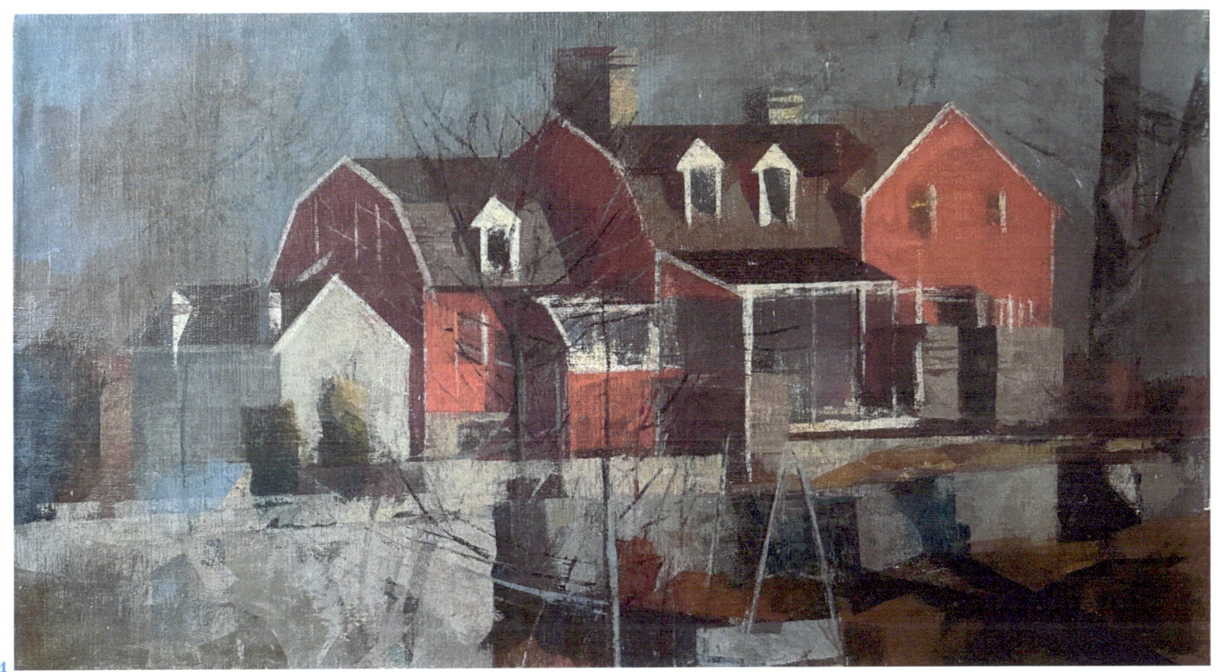

94

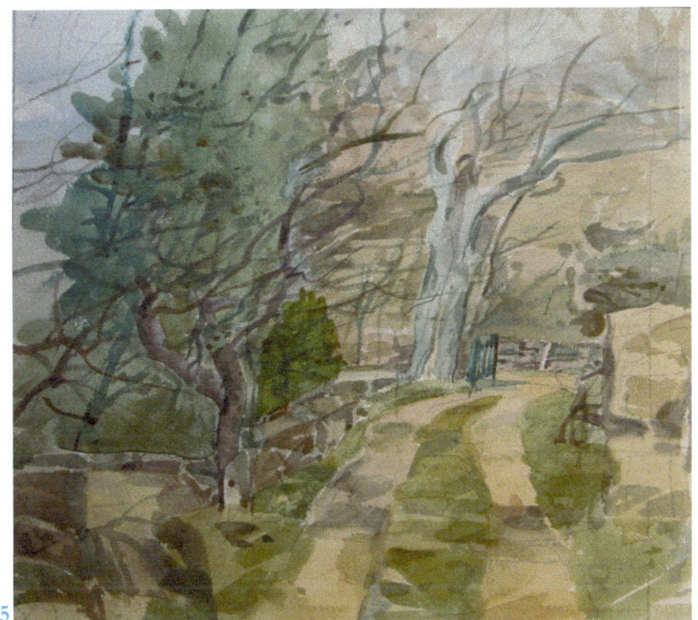

95

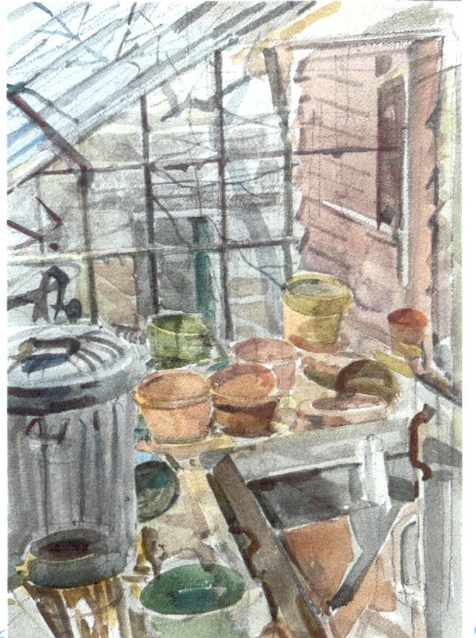

96

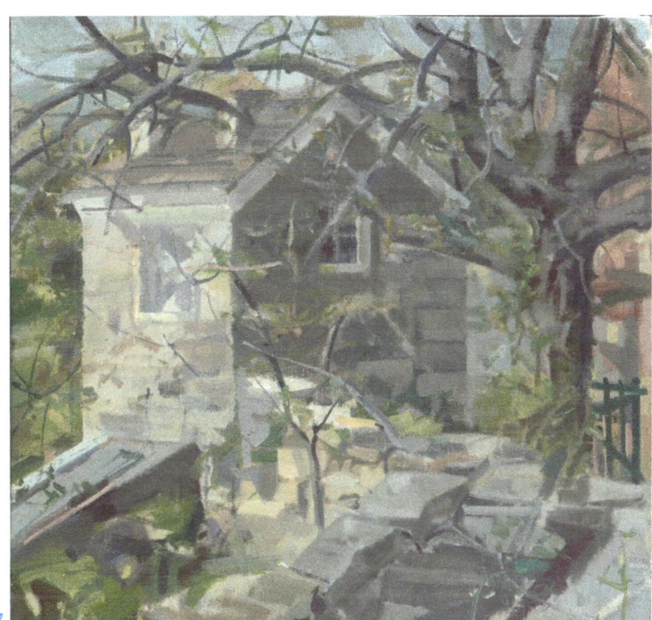

97

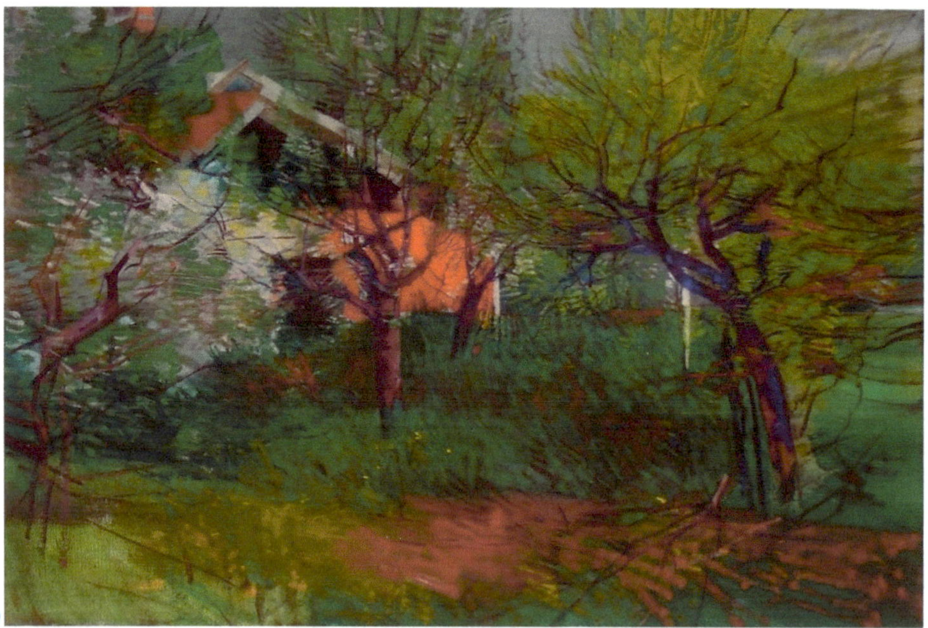

99

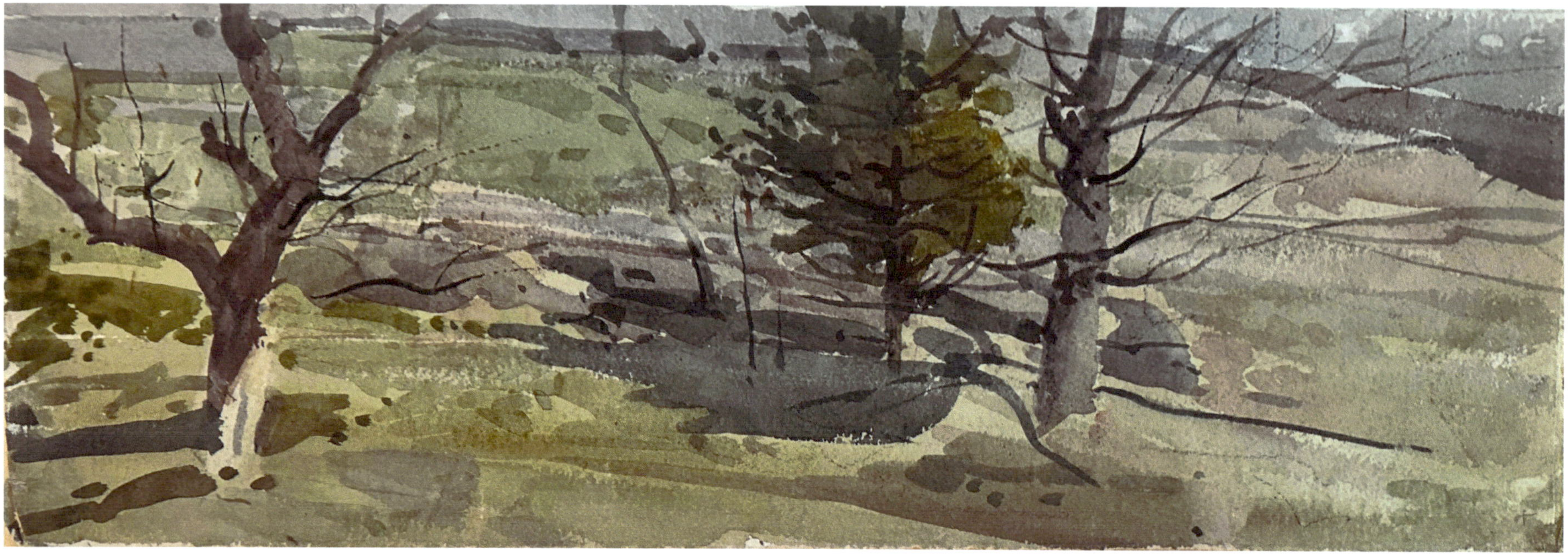

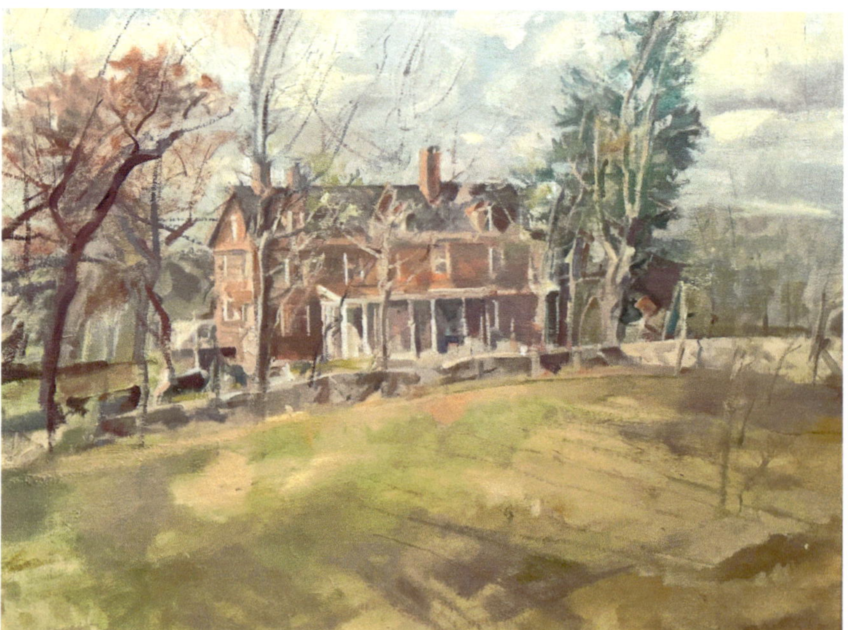

100

98

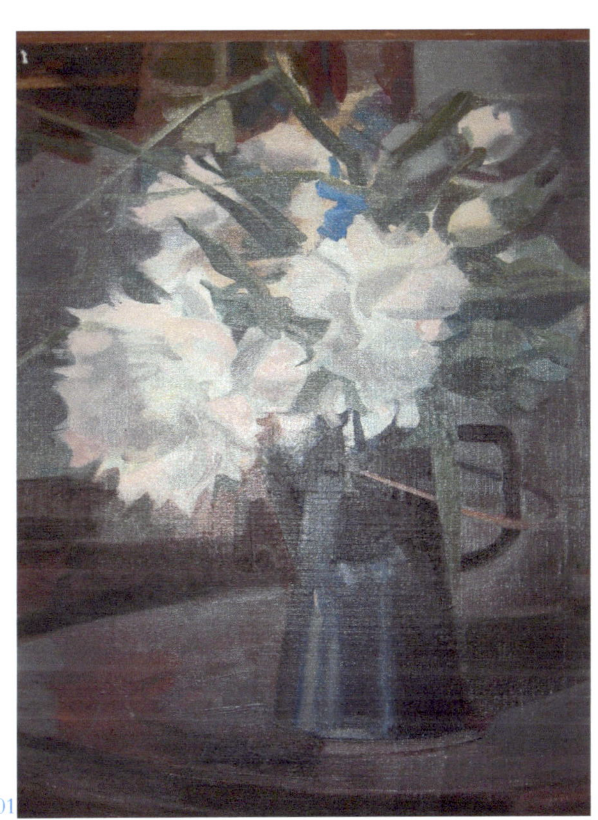

101

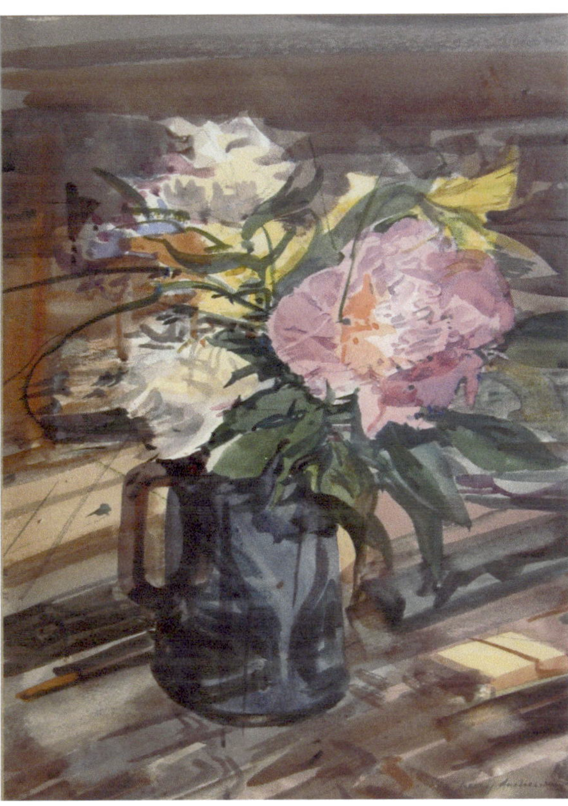

102

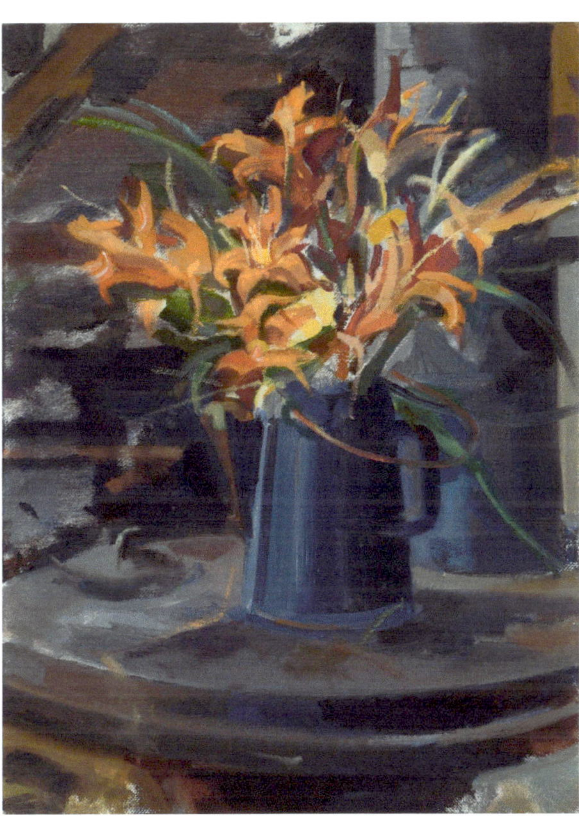

103

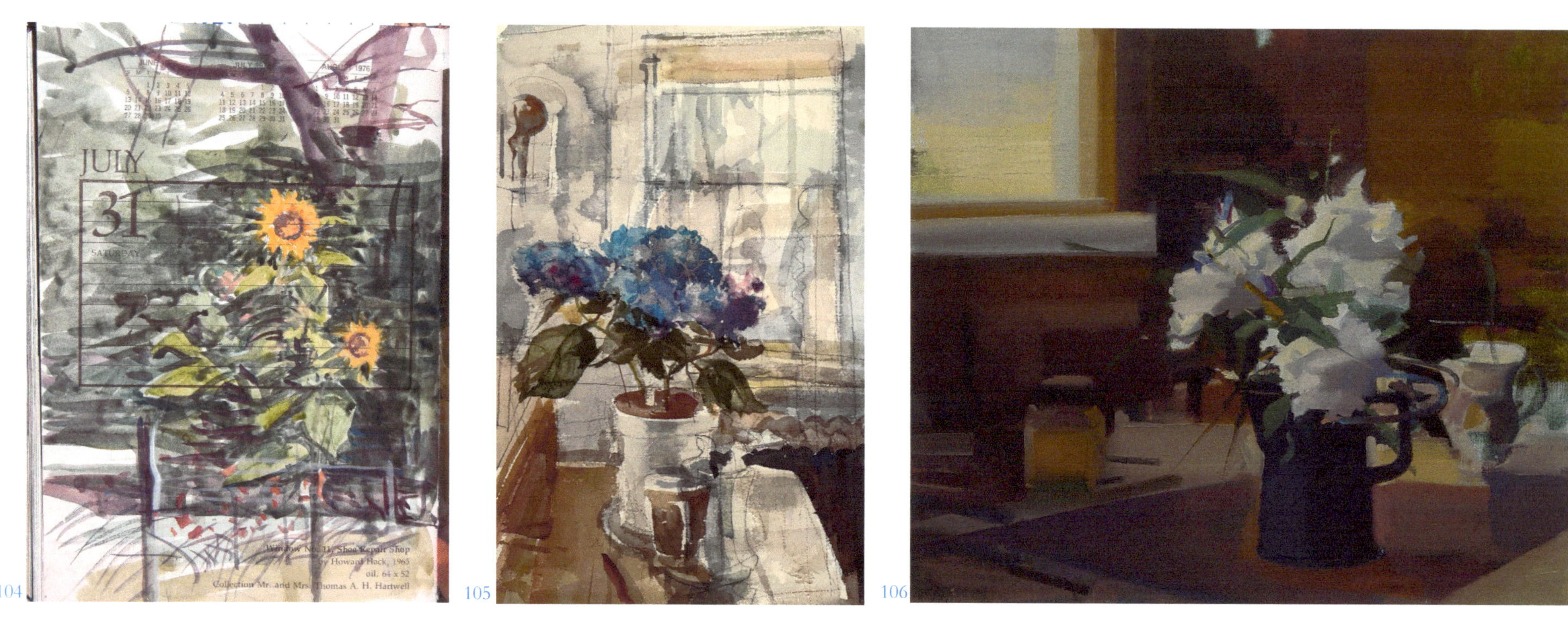

When you don't know where you're going the best thing is to stop and wait another time, and when you feel that you have an idea that you can improve something, that's a good time to work on it (VHS recording c. 1987).

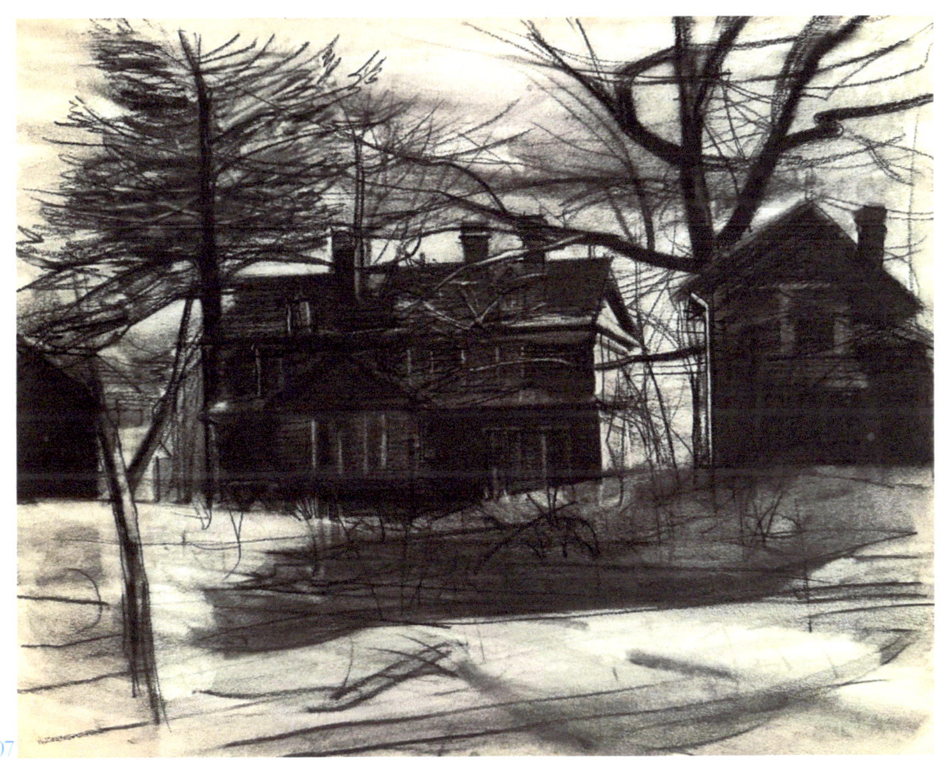

107

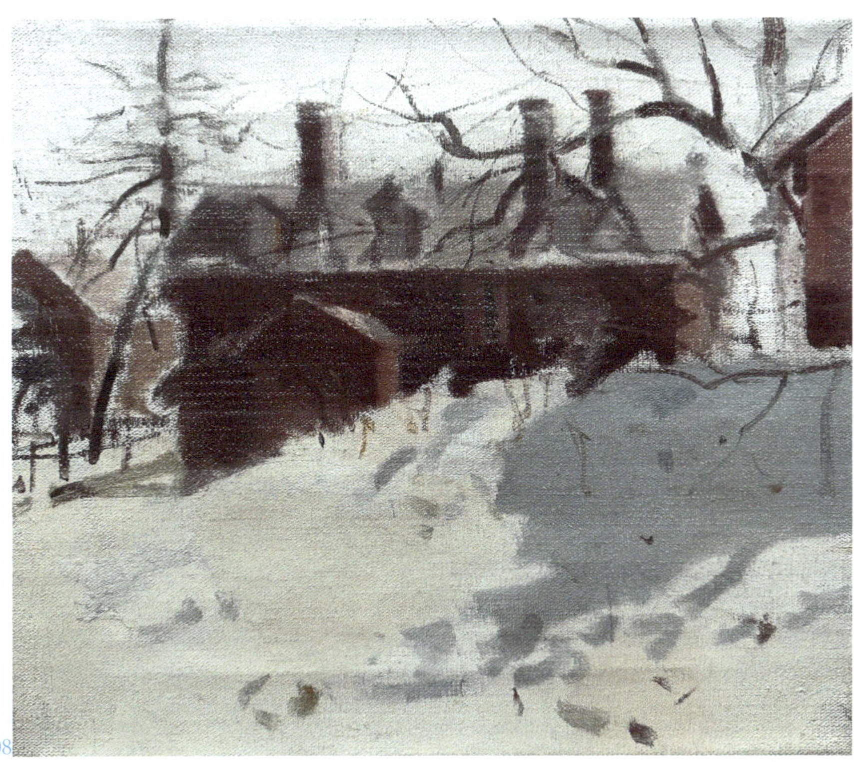

108

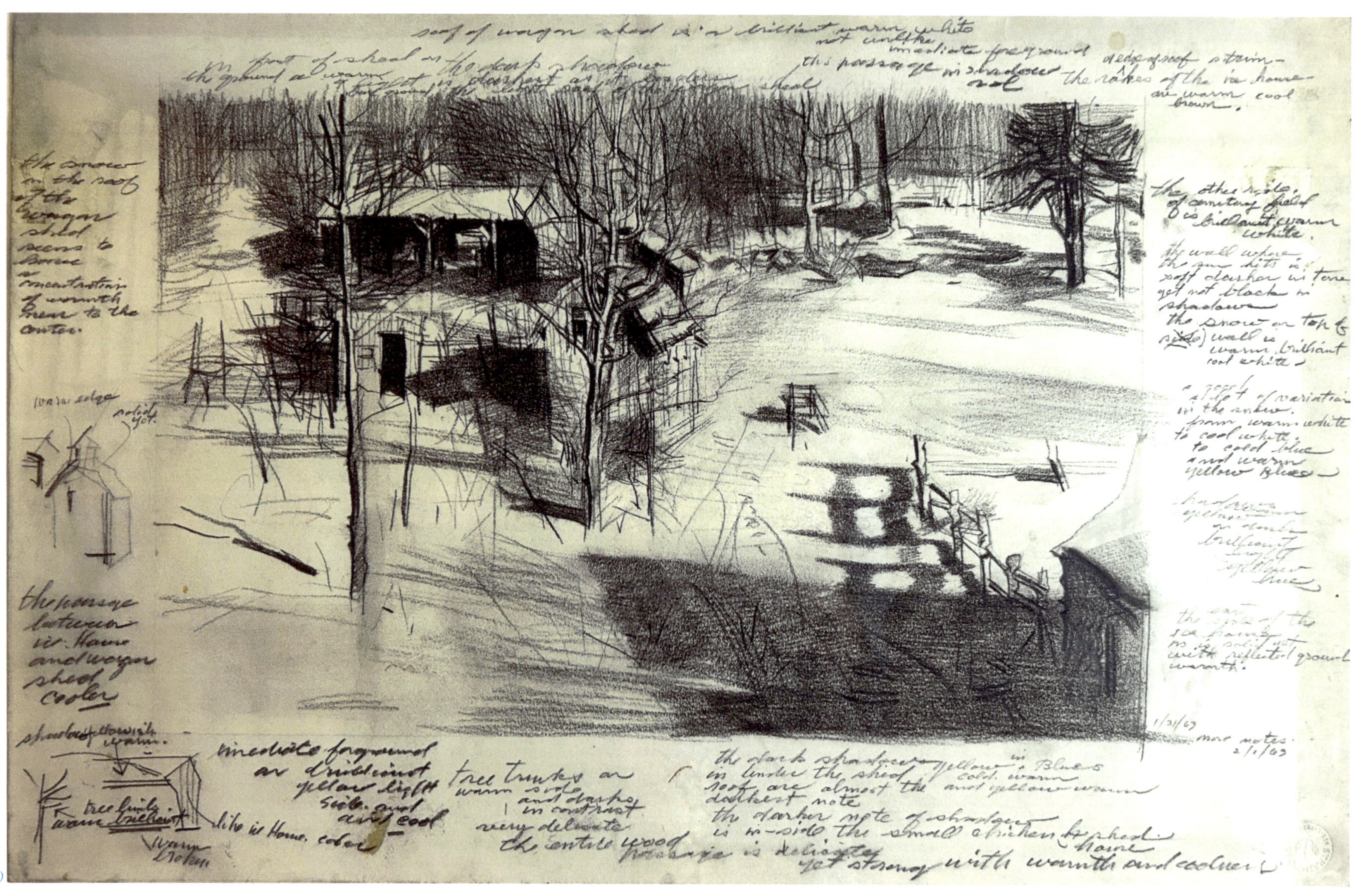

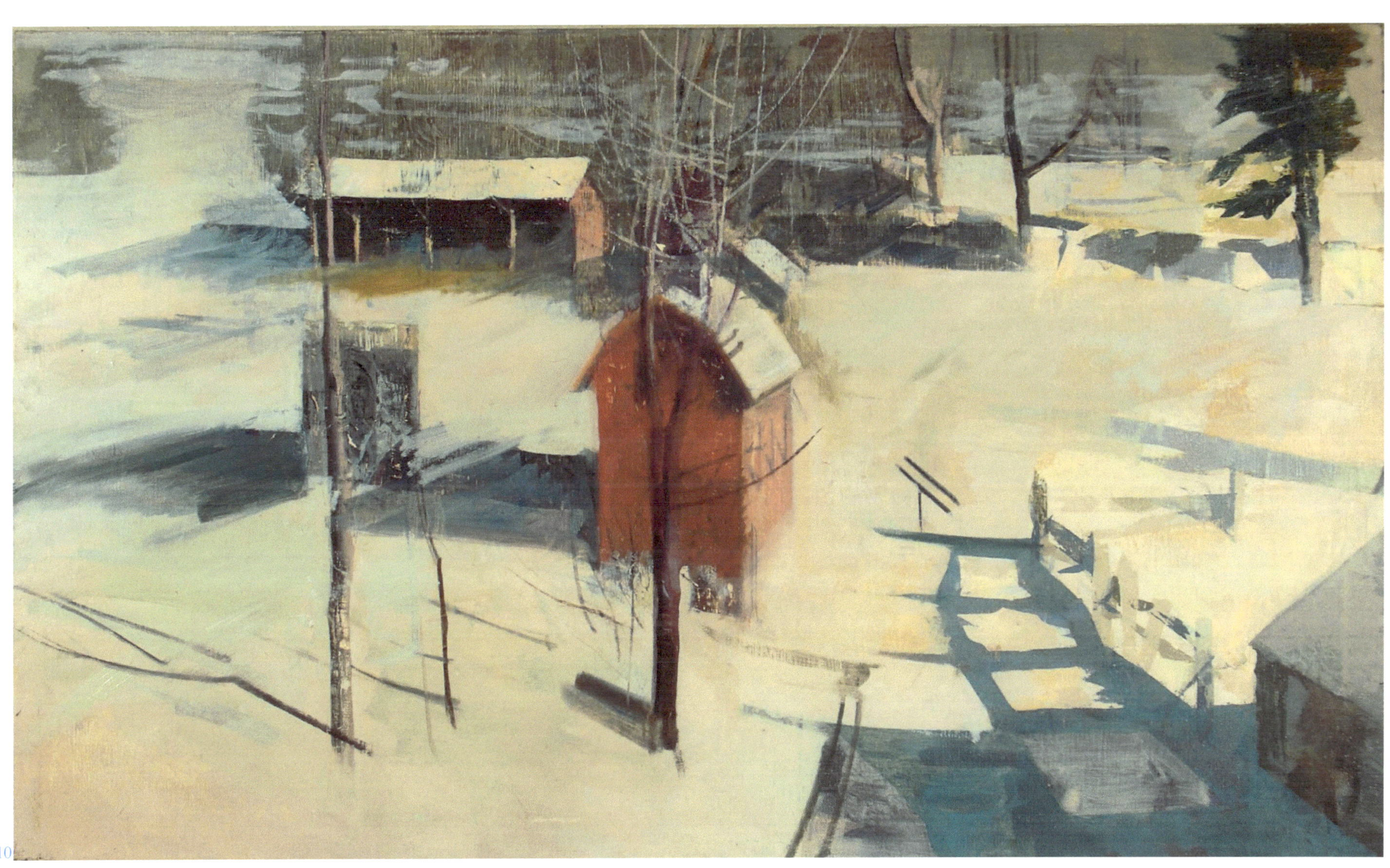

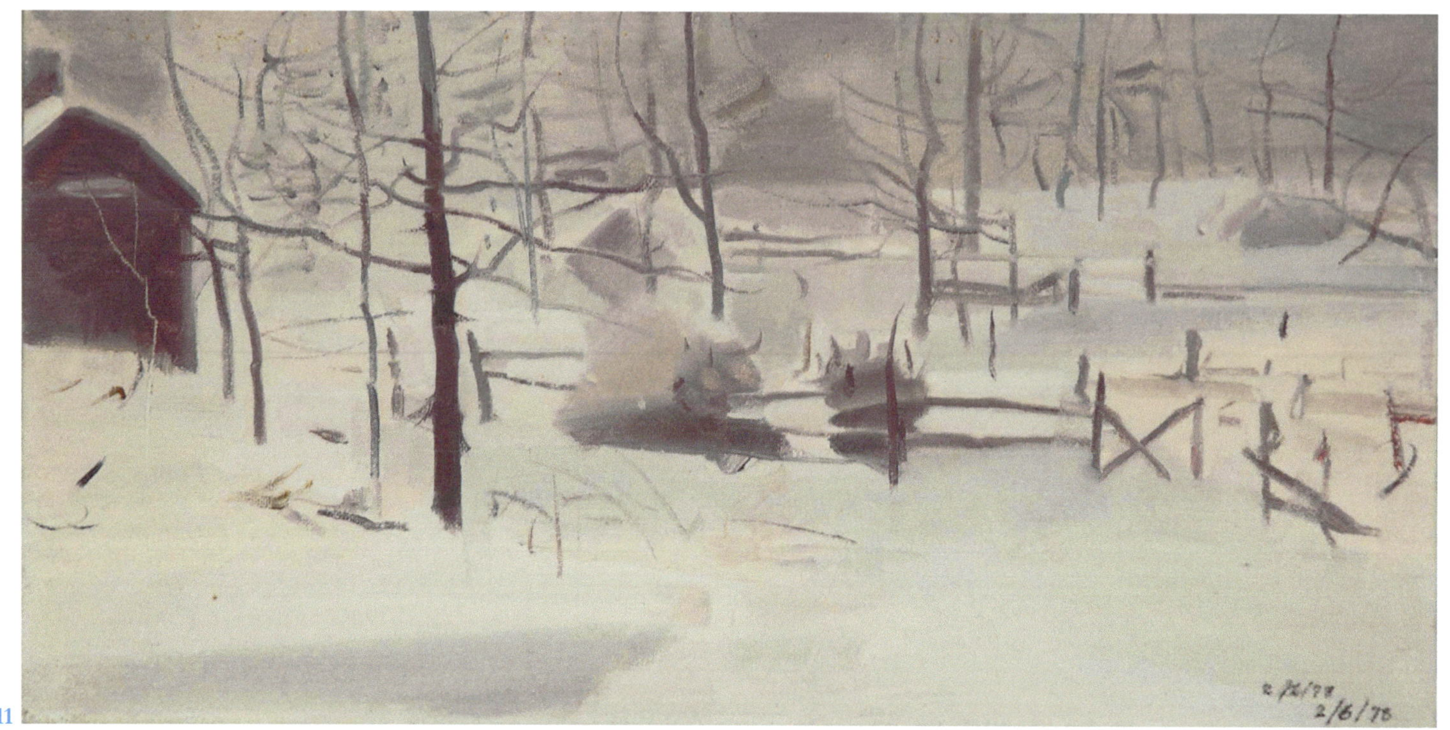

111

2/6/78

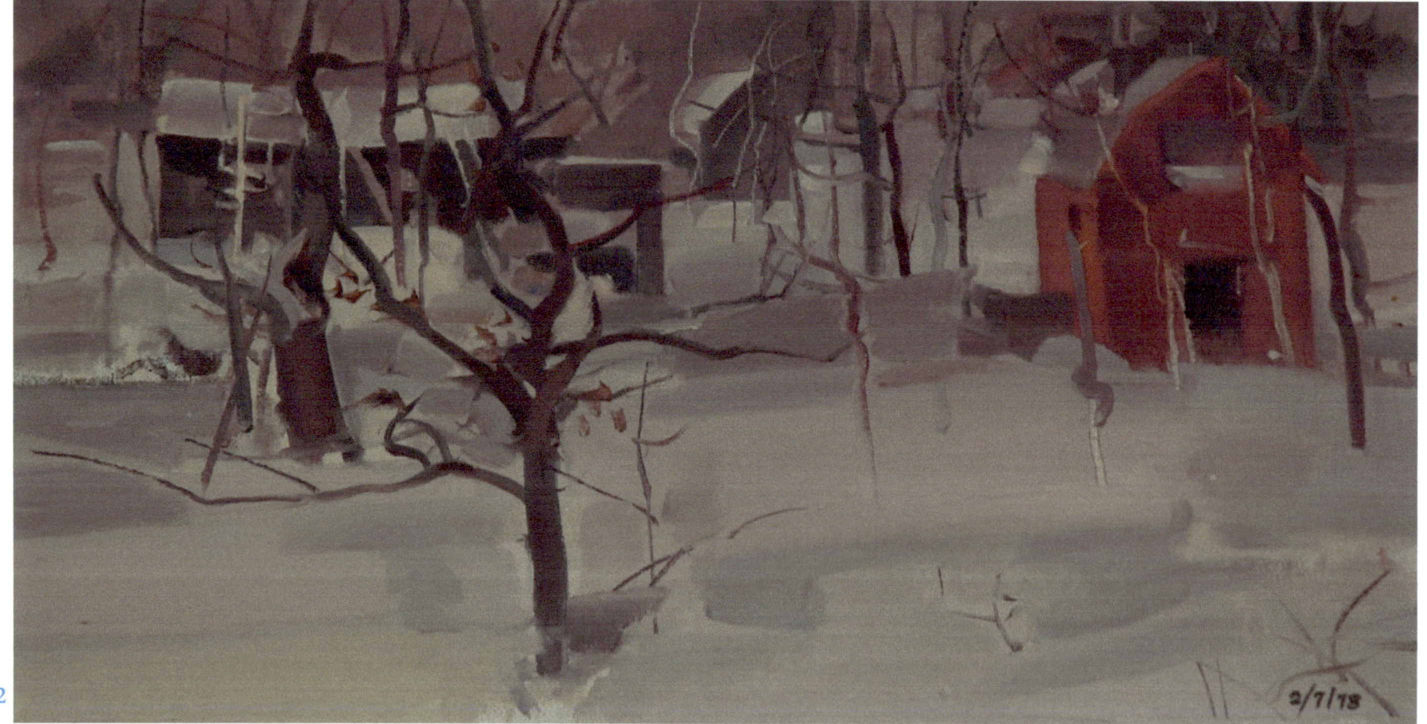

112

2/7/78

78

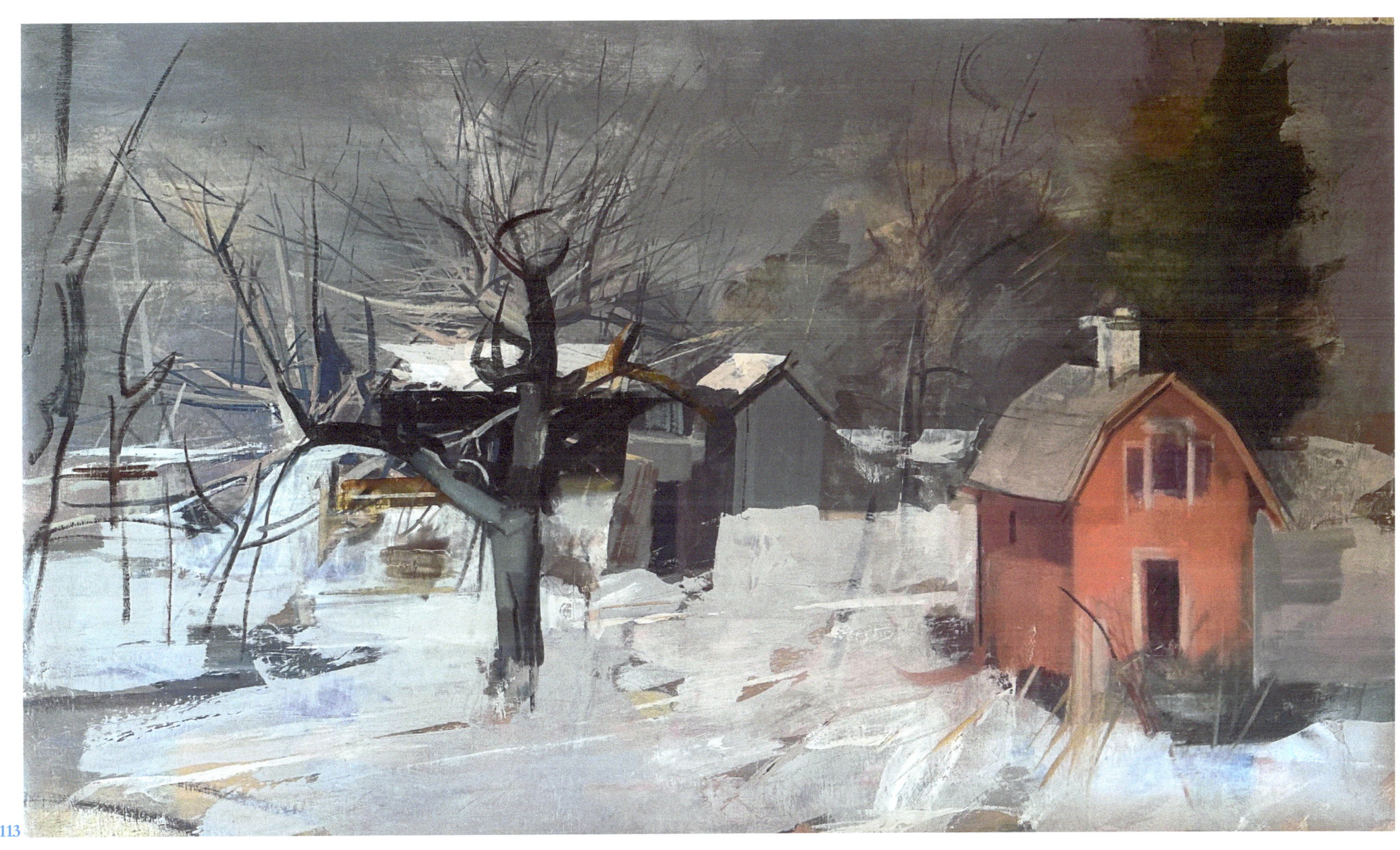

113

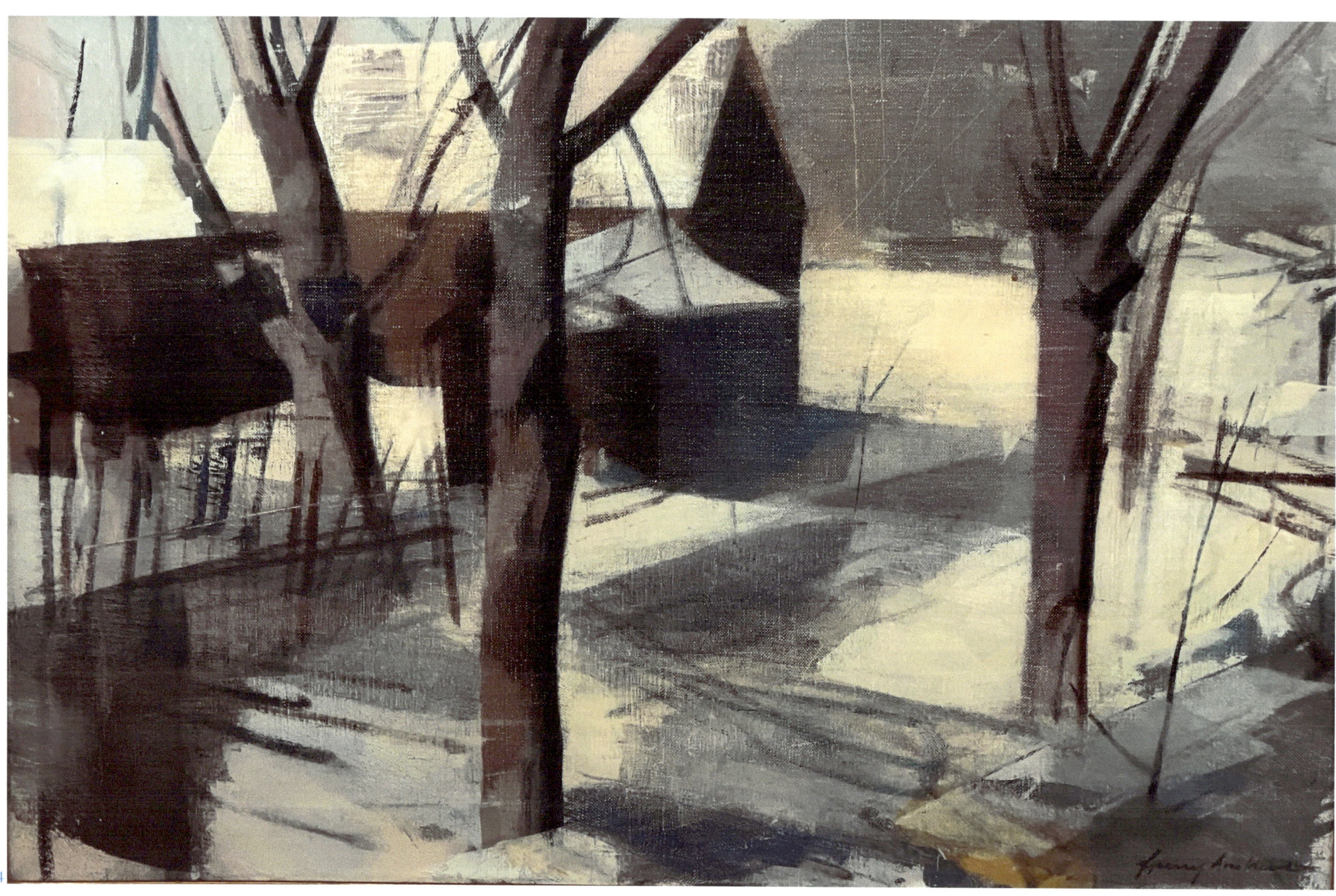

80

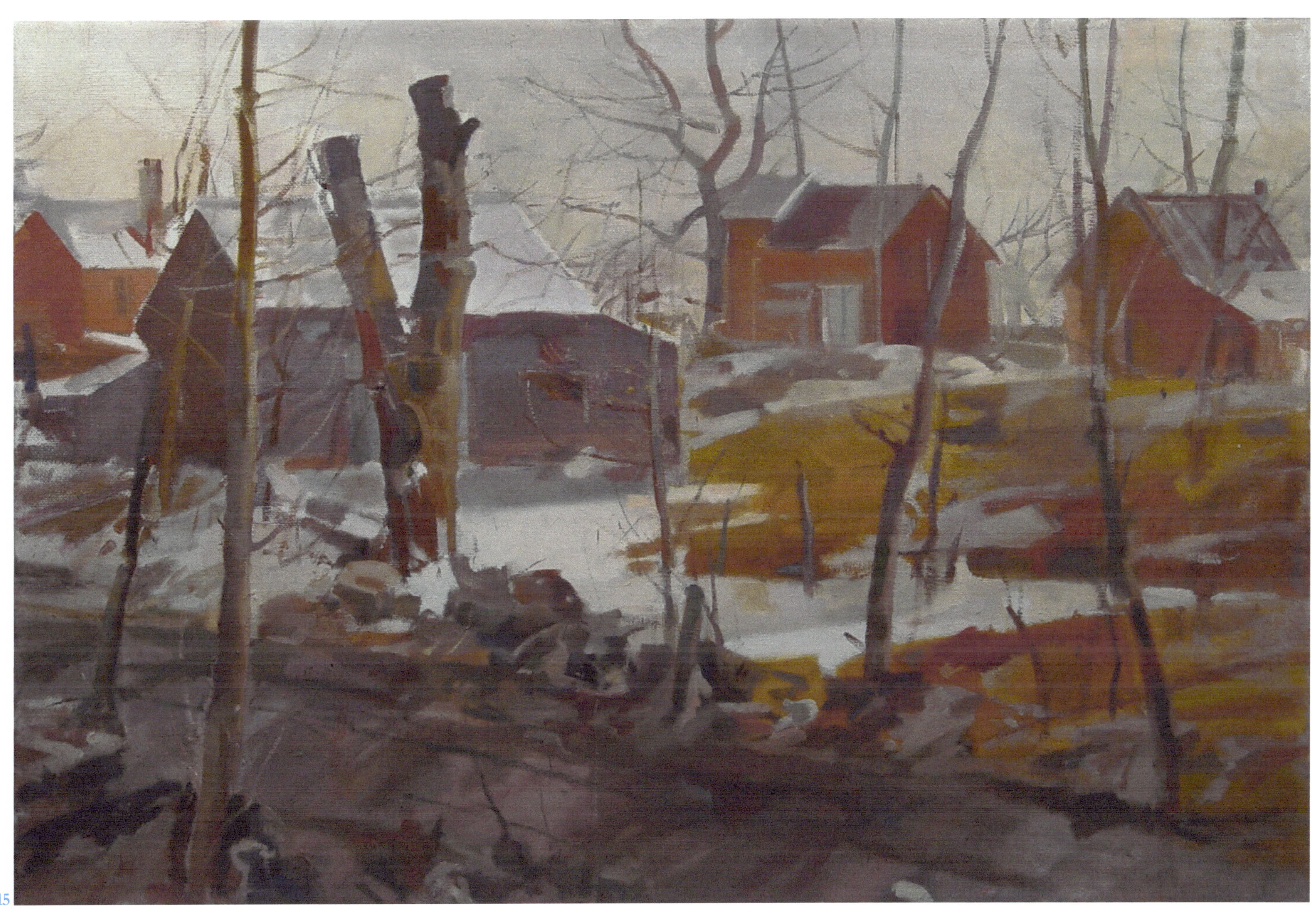

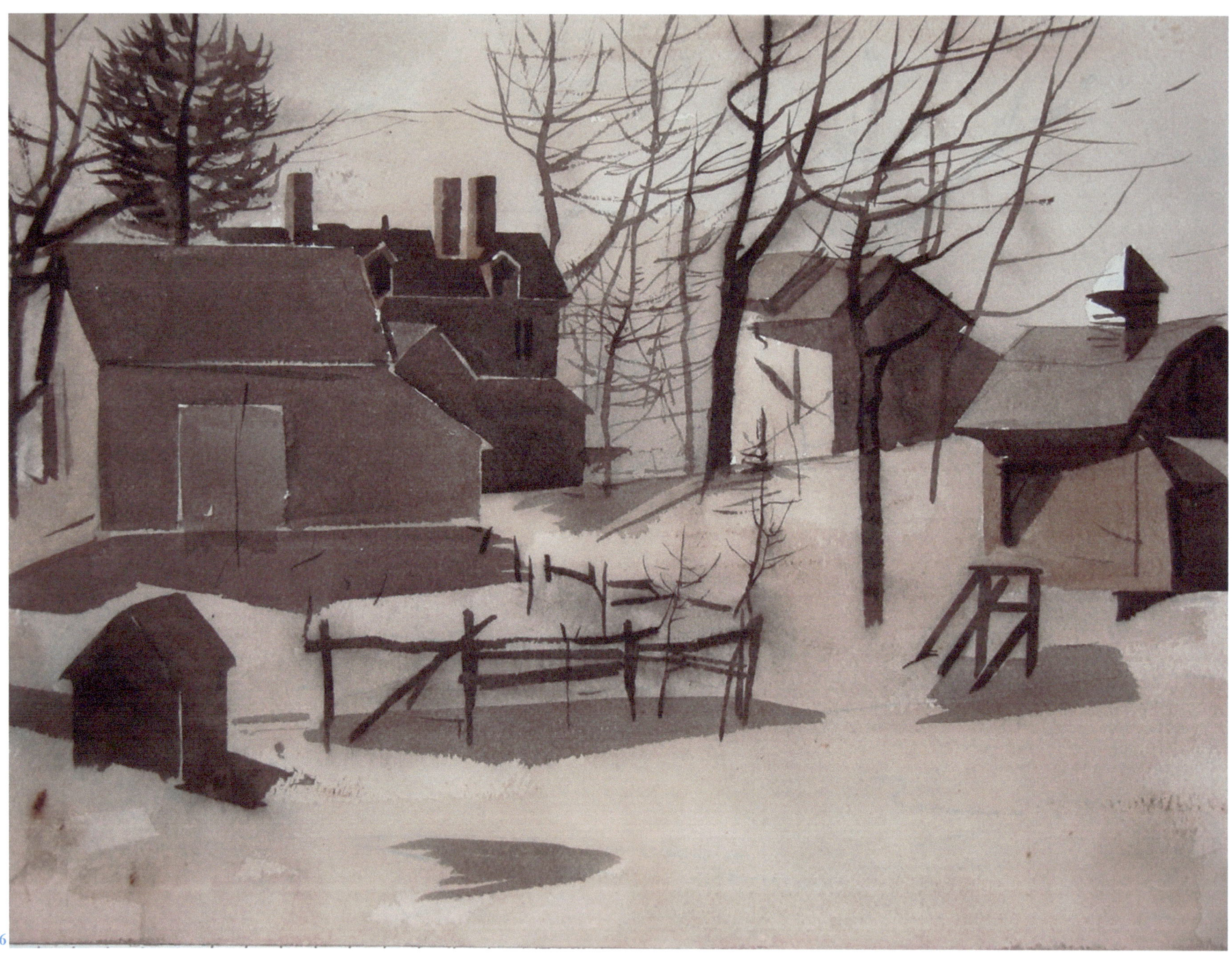

82

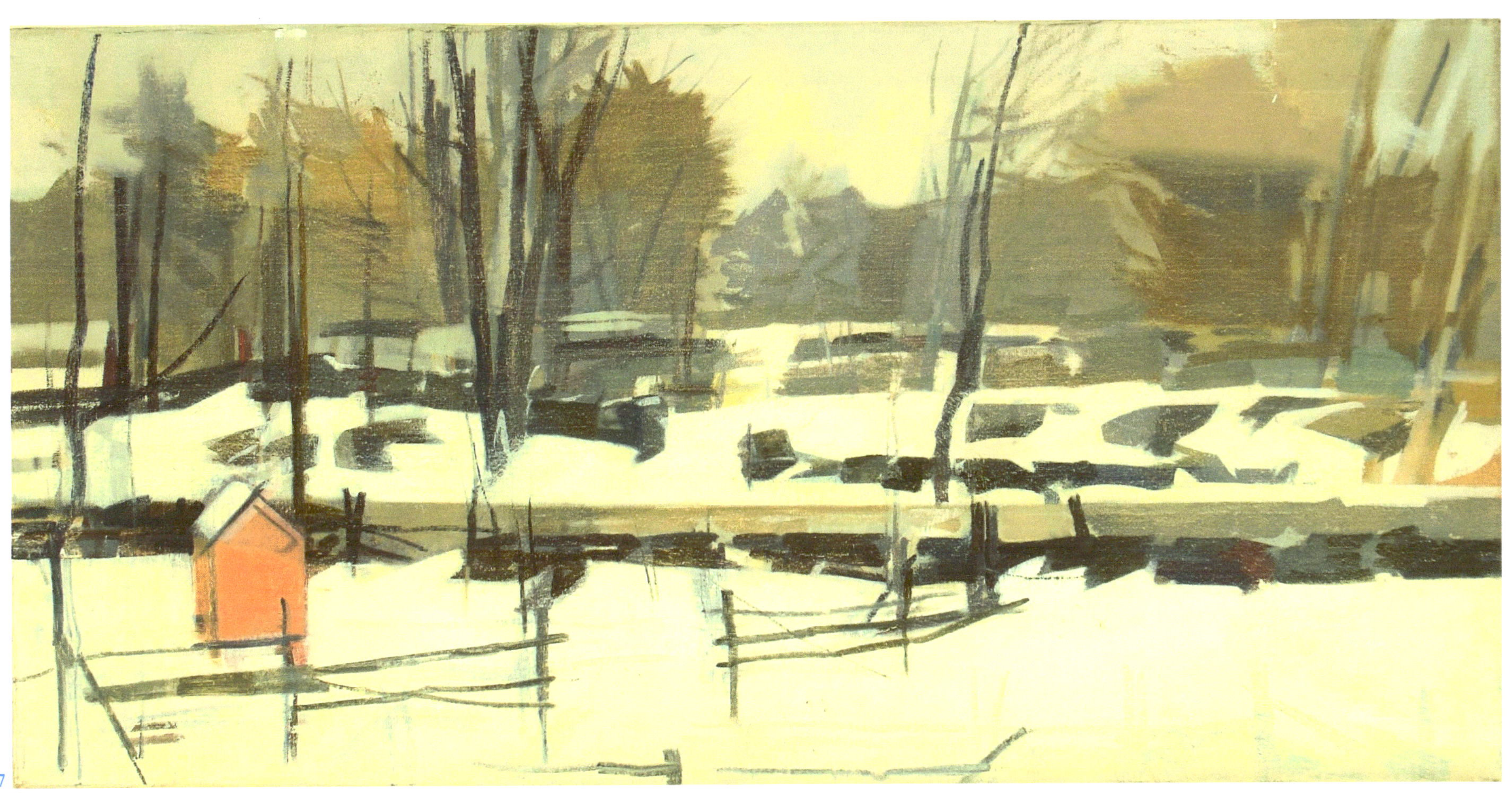

117

83

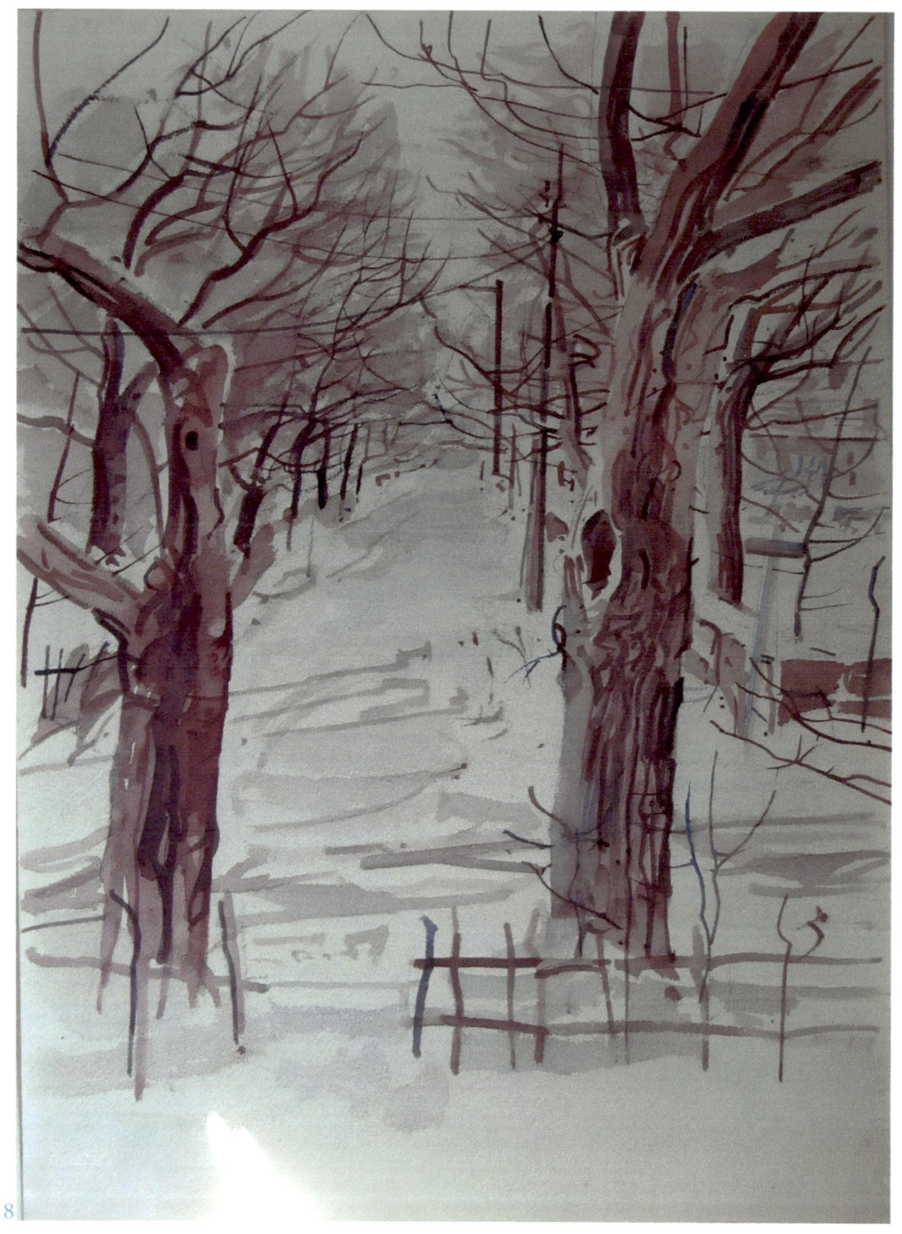

118

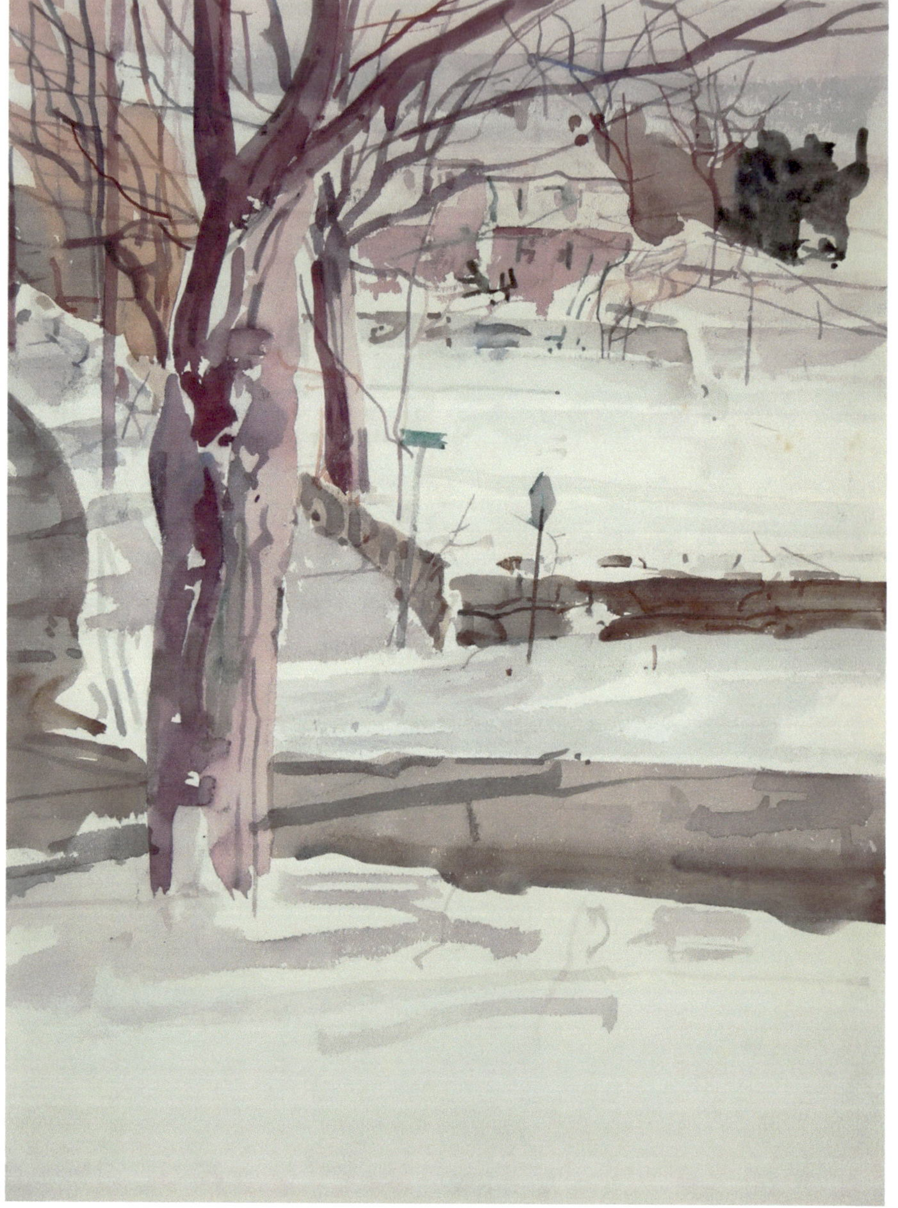

119

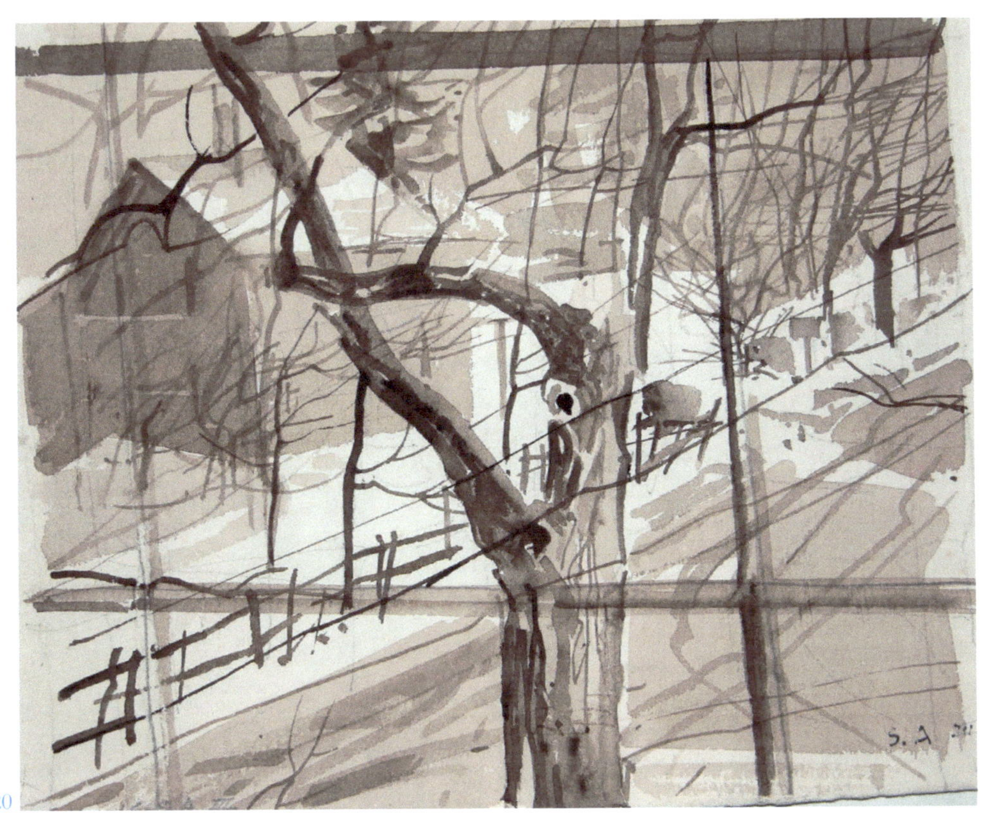

120

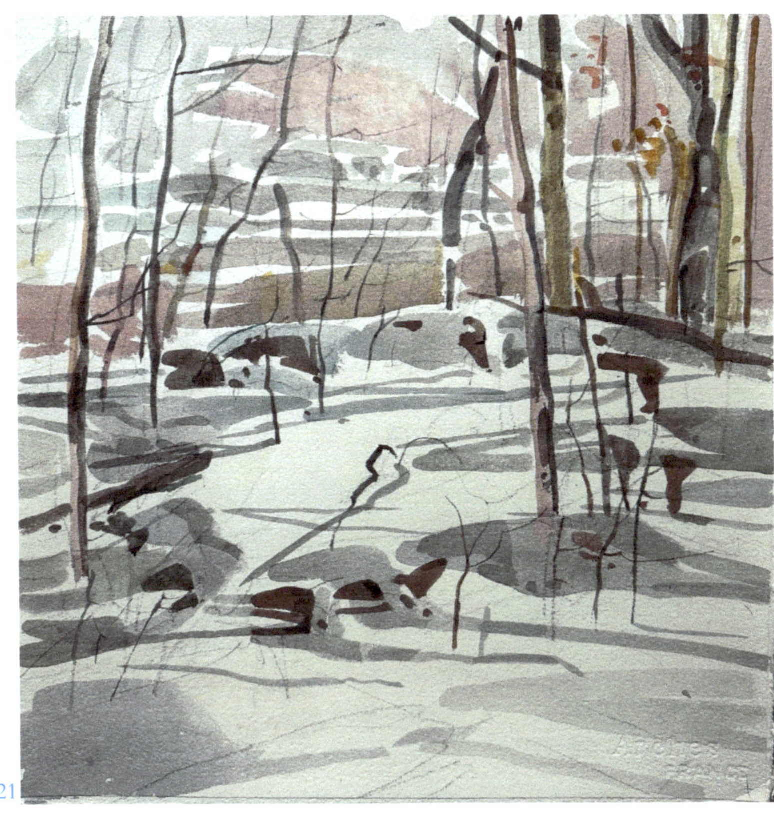

121

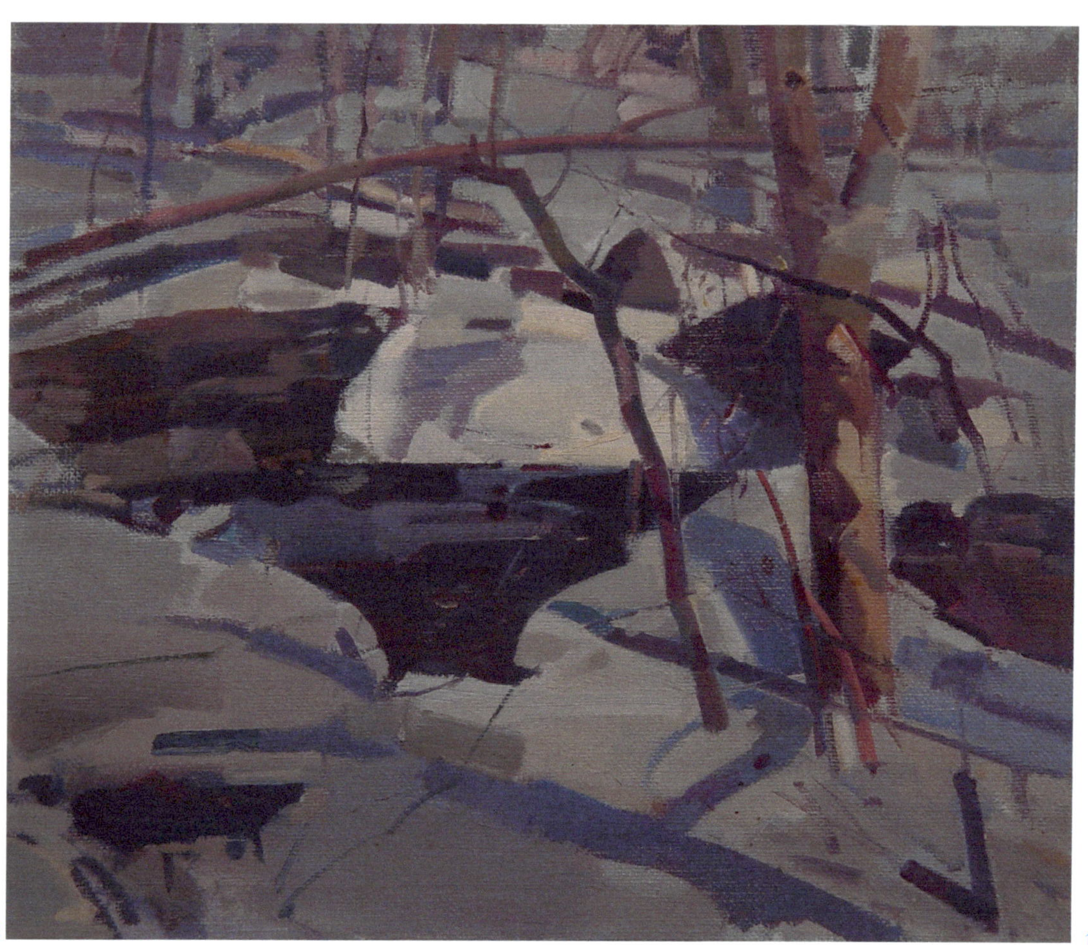

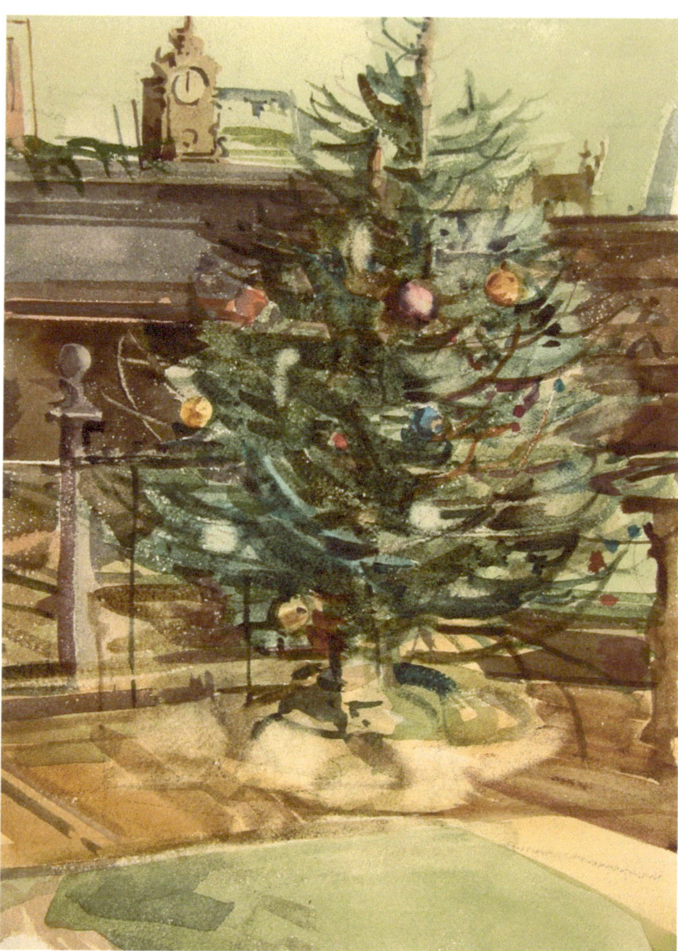

Whatever Sperry did in his own unique and inimitable manner in his art and in his personal life he always brought himself and he never needed to bring anything else (M. Young, eulogy, 2005).

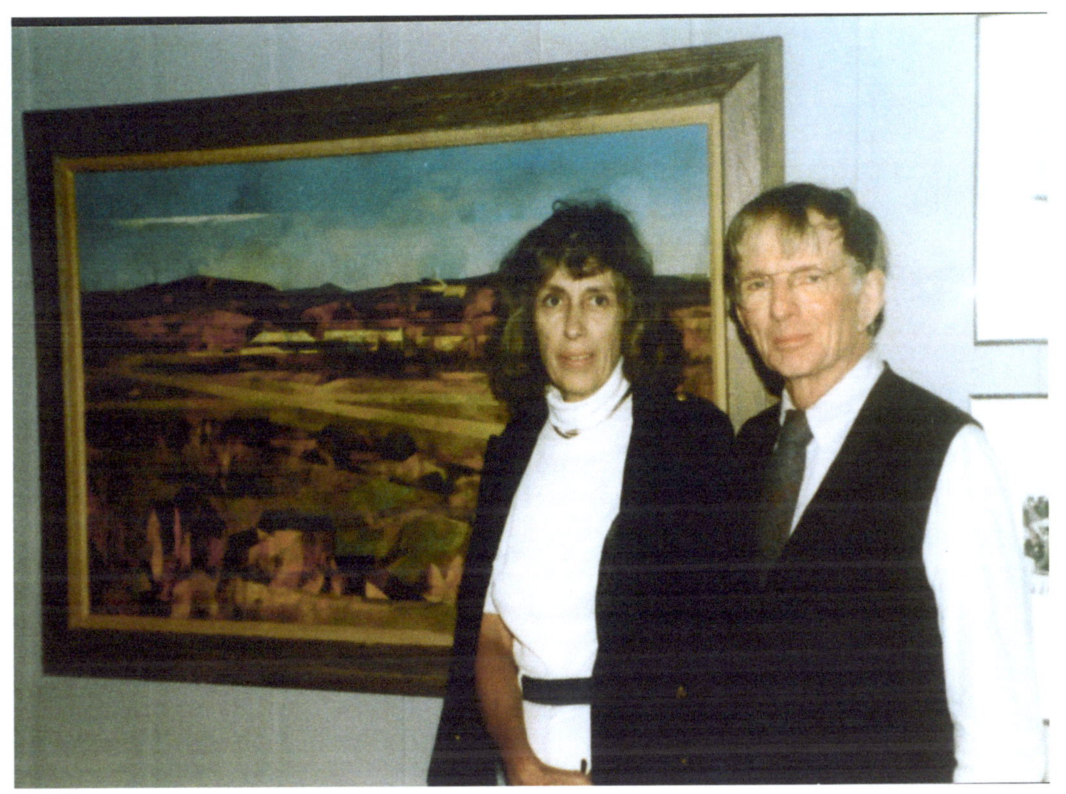
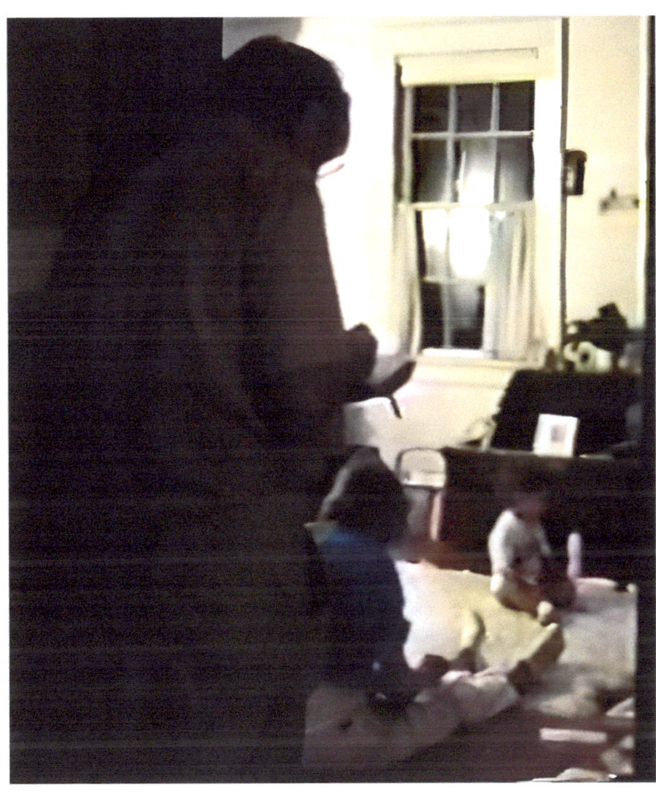

Sperry showed at the Century Club in New York. After the opening of the exhibition, we walked with him to Grand Central Station. He was all ready to take the train home to Connecticut. He had paintings under his arm. He stood apart among all of the harried New York commuters. He knew where he was going—home. Home to paint and home to Doris. He was dignified, genuine, loving and above all an artist. They both were. They had a great love for their family and friends and that love was returned to them by those of us who were fortunate enough to be called friends (C. Gibbons, personal communication, August 29 2005).

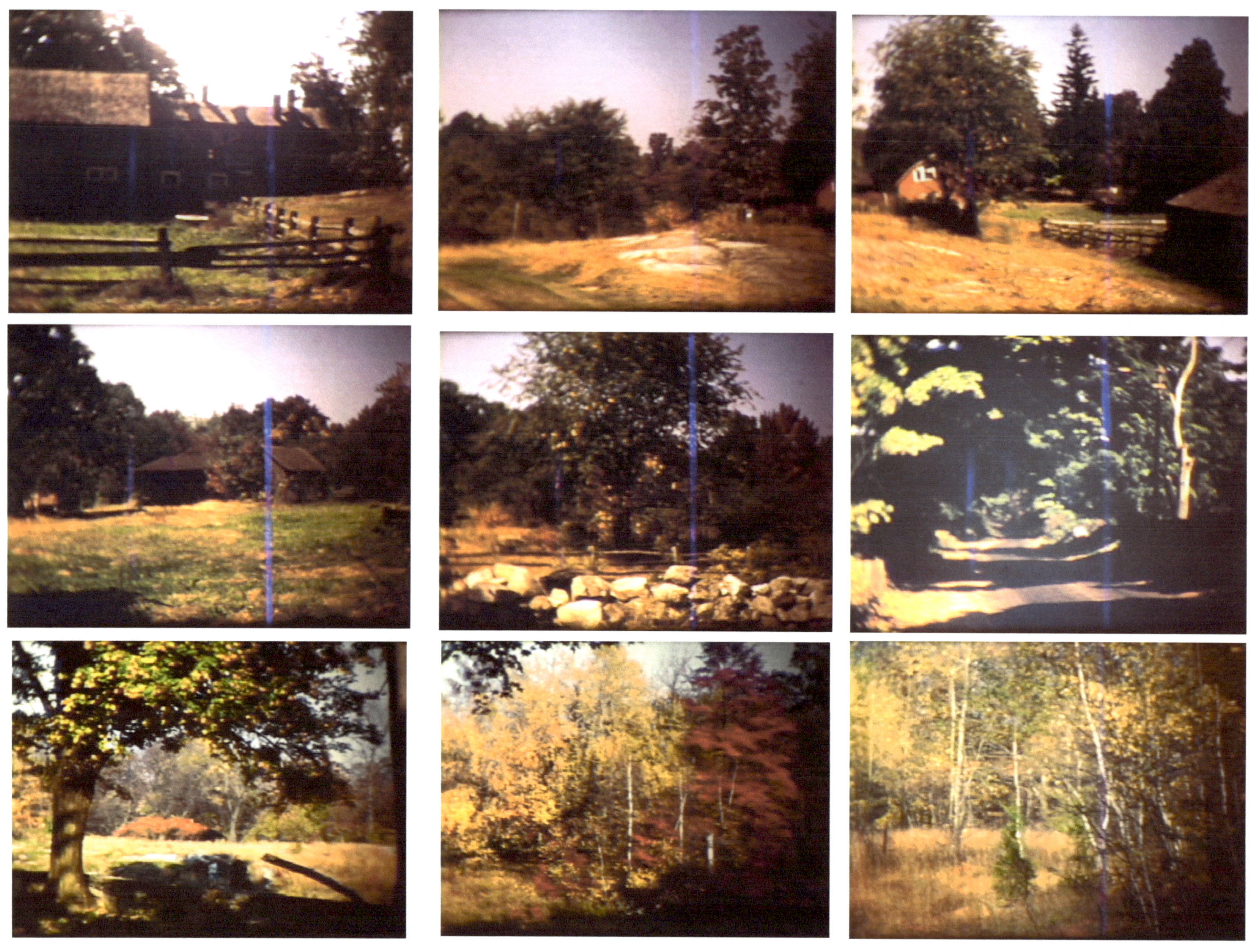

Frame grabs from home movies my mother took in the early 1960s with her wind up 1920s Bell and Howell camera on Kodachrome 16 mm film. Most structures depicted in my father's paintings are still standing, with the exception of the wagon shed and boat house (pg. 53).

Charles Sperry Andrews III (b. 1917, d. 2005)

Exhibitions

National Academy of Design, New York, NY, Annual Exhibitions 1938, 1940, 1947, 1950, 1952, 1958, 1993
Ferargil Gallery, New York, NY, 1950, 1952 (solo), 1953 (solo)
Silvermine Guild 1950, 1951
St. Lawrence University 1952
Kipnis Gallery, 1954, 1955
Slater Memorial Museum, Norwich CT, 1956, Group Exhibition
Wadsworth Atheneum, Harford, CT, 1957, Group Exhibition
New Britain Museum of American Art, New Britain, CT, 1962, 1983
Larcada Gallery, New York, NY, 1966, 1969
Bethel Gallery, Bethel, CT, 1977
Katonah Gallery, Katonah NY, 1983
Lyme Academy Gallery, Old Lyme, CT, 1989
National Academy of Design, New York, NY. Group Exhibition, 1993
Weir Farm National Historic Site, Wilton, CT, 1993, 2006, 2014, 2017
Jessie Edwards Gallery, Block Island RI, 2011, 2012
Block Island Historical Society, Block Island RI 2012-2015
Wilton Library, Wilton CT, 2012

Honors and Awards

First Julius Hallgarten Prize, National Academy of Design, Annual Exhibition, New York, NY, 1950
Major Award, Annual All New England Exhibition, Silvermine Guild of Artists, 1951
First Prize, St. Lawrence Valley Exhibition, Canton, NY, 1952
William Bradford Green Memorial Prize for Landscape, Connecticut Academy of Fine Arts, 1954, 1956
Salmagundi Club Award for a U.S. Citizen, Audubon Artist, 20th Annual Exhibit, New York, NY, 1962
Award, Connecticut Academy of Fine Arts, 1969
Certificate of Merit, National Academy of Design, New York, NY, 1978
John Pike Memorial Award, 163rd Annual Exhibition, National Academy of Design, New York, NY, 1988
Century Association, New York, NY, 1993
Associate National Academician, National Academy of Design, New York, NY, 1990
National Academician, National Academy of Design, New York, NY, 1994

Collections

American Academy and Institute of Arts and Letters, New York, NY

Columbus Gallery of Fine Arts, Columbus, OH

Wadsworth Atheneum, Harford, CT

New Britain Museum of American Art, New Britain, CT

National Academy of Design, New York, NY

Miami University Art Museum, Oxford, OH

Weir Farm National Historical Park, Wilton, CT

Bibliography

Connecticut Contemporary Painting 1951

"Sperry Andrews," American Artist Magazine, 1952

"Painting at the Site of American Impressionism," American Artist Magazine, 1993

Studies

The National Academy of Design, New York, NY, 1933-1936

The Art Students League, New York, NY, (1946-1948 approx.)

Teaching

Silvermine School of the Arts, Westport, CT

Wooster Community Arts Center, Danbury, CT

Further information:

https://www.nps.gov/wefa/learn/historyculture/sperryandrews.htm

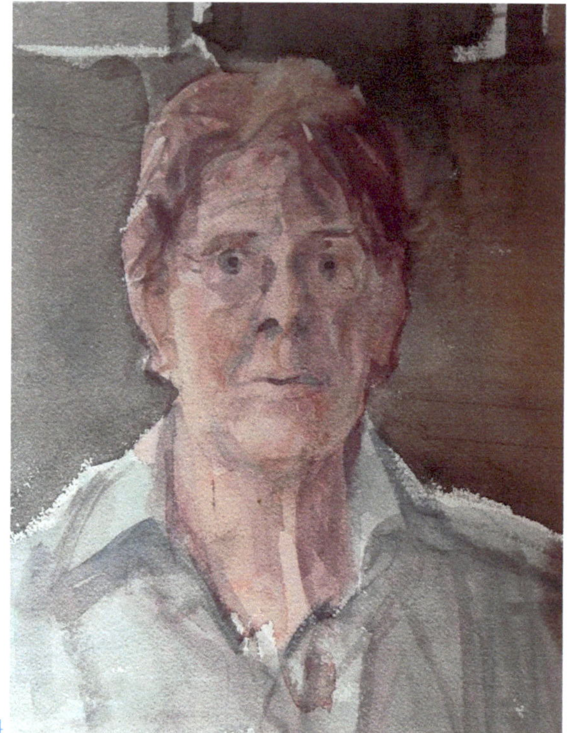
124

Index of paintings:

Abbreviations:
O/C Oil on Canvas
WC Watercolor
G/C Graphite and/or charcoal
P/I Pen & Ink
C Charcoal
E Etching
O/B Oil on Board
Mono. Monochrome
NPS National Park Service